Harvard
Business
Review

ON
WHAT MAKES A LEADER

D0172632

THE HARVARD BUSINESS REVIEW PAPERBACK SERIES

The series is designed to bring today's managers and professionals the fundamental information they need to stay competitive in a fast-moving world. From the preeminent thinkers whose work has defined an entire field to the rising stars who will redefine the way we think about business, here are the leading minds and landmark ideas that have established the *Harvard Business Review* as required reading for ambitious businesspeople in organizations around the globe.

Other books in the series:

Other books in the series (continued):

Harvard Business Review on Managing the Value Chain

Harvard Business Review on Measuring Corporate Performance

Harvard Business Review on Mergers and Acquisitions

Harvard Business Review on Negotiation and Conflict Resolution

Harvard Business Review on Nonprofits

Harvard Business Review on Organizational Learning

Harvard Business Review on Strategies for Growth

Harvard Business Review on Turnarounds

Harvard Business Review on Work and Life Balance

Harvard Business Review

ON

WHAT MAKES A LEADER

A HARVARD BUSINESS REVIEW PAPERBACK

Copyright 1998, 1999, 2000, 2001
Harvard Business School Publishing Corporation
All rights reserved
Printed in the United States of America
05 04 03 02 01   5 4 3 2 1

All rights reserved. No part of this book may be reproduced, stored in a retrieval system, or transmitted, in any form or by any means, electronic, mechanical, photocopying, recording, or otherwise without the prior written permission of the copyright holder.

The *Harvard Business Review* articles in this collection are available as individual reprints. Discounts apply to quantity purchases. For information and ordering, please contact Customer Service, Harvard Business School Publishing, Boston, MA 02163. Telephone: (617) 783-7500 or (800) 988-0886, 8 A.M. to 6 P.M. Eastern Time, Monday through Friday. Fax: (617) 783-7555, 24 hours a day. E-mail: custserv@hbsp.harvard.edu

Library of Congress Cataloging-in-Publication Data
Harvard business review on what makes a leader.
     p.   cm. — (A Harvard business review paperback)
    Includes bibliographical references and index.
    ISBN 1-57851-637-4 (alk. paper)
    1. Leadership. 2. Executive ability. 3. Industrial management. 4. Management. I. Title: What makes a leader. II. Harvard business review. III. Harvard business review paperback series.
HD57.7.H388   2001
658.4'092—dc21   2001039412
                                                                CIP

The paper used in this publication meets the requirements of the American National Standard for Permanence of Paper for Publications and Documents in Libraries and Archives Z39.48-1992.

Contents

Harvard
Business
Review

ON
WHAT MAKES A LEADER

What Makes a Leader?

DANIEL GOLEMAN

Executive Summary

SUPERB LEADERS HAVE very different ways of directing
a team, a division, or a company. Some are subdued
and analytical; others are charismatic and go with their
gut. And different situations call for different types of leadership. Most mergers need a sensitive negotiator at the
helm, whereas many turnarounds require a more forceful
kind of authority.

Psychologist and noted author Daniel Goleman has
found, however, that effective leaders are alike in one
crucial way: they all have a high degree of what has
come to be known as *emotional intelligence*. In fact,
Goleman's research at nearly 200 large, global companies revealed that emotional intelligence—especially at
the highest levels of a company—is the sine qua non for
leadership. Without it, a person can have first-class training, an incisive mind, and an endless supply of good
ideas, but he still won't make a great leader.

The components of emotional intelligence—self-aware-ness, self-regulation, motivation, empathy, and social skill—can sound unbusinesslike. But exhibiting emotional intelligence at the workplace does not mean simply con-trolling your anger or getting along with people. Rather, it means understanding your own and other people's emotional makeup well enough to move people in the direction of accomplishing your company's goals.

In this article, the author discusses each component of emotional intelligence and shows through examples how to recognize it in potential leaders, how and why it leads to measurable business results, and how it can be learned. It takes time and, most of all, commitment. But the benefits that come from having a well-developed emotional intelligence, both for the individual and the organization, make it worth the effort.

EVERY BUSINESSPERSON knows a story about a highly intelligent, highly skilled executive who was pro-moted into a leadership position only to fail at the job. And they also know a story about someone with solid—but not extraordinary—intellectual abilities and techni-cal skills who was promoted into a similar position and then soared.

Such anecdotes support the widespread belief that identifying individuals with the "right stuff" to be leaders is more art than science. After all, the personal styles of superb leaders vary: some leaders are subdued and ana-lytical; others shout their manifestos from the mountain-tops. And just as important, different situations call for different types of leadership. Most mergers need a sensi-tive negotiator at the helm, whereas many turnarounds require a more forceful authority.

I have found, however, that the most effective leaders are alike in one crucial way: they all have a high degree of what has come to be known as *emotional intelligence*. It's not that IQ and technical skills are irrelevant. They do matter, but mainly as "threshold capabilities"; that is,

Effective leaders are alike in one crucial way: they all have a high degree of emotional intelligence.

they are the entry-level requirements for executive positions. But my research, along with other recent studies, clearly shows that emotional intelligence is the sine qua non of leadership. Without it, a person can have the best training in the world, an incisive, analytical mind, and an endless supply of smart ideas, but he still won't make a great leader.

In the course of the past year, my colleagues and I have focused on how emotional intelligence operates at work. We have examined the relationship between emotional intelligence and effective performance, especially in leaders. And we have observed how emotional intelligence shows itself on the job. How can you tell if someone has high emotional intelligence, for example, and how can you recognize it in yourself? In the following pages, we'll explore these questions, taking each of the components of emotional intelligence—self-awareness, self-regulation, motivation, empathy, and social skill—in turn.

Evaluating Emotional Intelligence

Most large companies today have employed trained psychologists to develop what are known as "competency models" to aid them in identifying, training, and promoting likely stars in the leadership firmament. The psychologists have also developed such models for lower-level positions. And in recent years, I have analyzed competency models from 188 companies, most of which were large and global and included the likes of Lucent Technologies, British Airways, and Credit Suisse.

In carrying out this work, my objective was to determine which personal capabilities drove outstanding performance within these organizations, and to what degree they did so. I grouped capabilities into three categories: purely technical skills like accounting and business planning; cognitive abilities like analytical reasoning; and competencies demonstrating emotional intelligence such as the ability to work with others and effectiveness in leading change.

To create some of the competency models, psychologists asked senior managers at the companies to identify the capabilities that typified the organization's most outstanding leaders. To create other models, the psychologists used objective criteria such as a division's profitability to differentiate the star performers at senior levels within their organizations from the average ones. Those individuals were then extensively interviewed and tested, and their capabilities were compared. This process resulted in the creation of lists of ingredients for highly effective leaders. The lists ranged in length from 7 to 15 items and included such ingredients as initiative and strategic vision.

When I analyzed all this data, I found dramatic results. To be sure, intellect was a driver of outstanding performance. Cognitive skills such as big-picture thinking and long-term vision were particularly important. But when I calculated the ratio of technical skills, IQ, and emotional intelligence as ingredients of excellent performance, emotional intelligence proved to be twice as important as the others for jobs at all levels.

Moreover, my analysis showed that emotional intelligence played an increasingly important role at the highest levels of the company, where differences in technical skills are of negligible importance. In other words, the higher the rank of a person considered to be a star performer, the more emotional intelligence capabilities showed up as the reason for his or her effectiveness. When I compared star performers with average ones in senior leadership positions, nearly 90% of the difference in their profiles was attributable to emotional intelligence factors rather than cognitive abilities.

Other researchers have confirmed that emotional intelligence not only distinguishes outstanding leaders but can also be linked to strong performance. The findings of the late David McClelland, the renowned researcher in human and organizational behavior, are a good example. In a 1996 study of a global food and beverage company, McClelland found that when senior managers had a critical mass of emotional intelligence capabilities, their divisions outperformed yearly earnings goals by 20%. Meanwhile, division leaders without that critical mass underperformed by almost the same amount. McClelland's findings, interestingly, held as true in the company's U.S. divisions as in its divisions in Asia and Europe.

In short, the numbers are beginning to tell us a persuasive story about the link between a company's success and the emotional intelligence of its leaders. And just as important, research is also demonstrating that people can, if they take the right approach, develop their emotional intelligence. (See the insert "Can Emotional Intelligence Be Learned?")

Self-Awareness

Self-awareness is the first component of emotional intelligence—which makes sense when one considers that the Delphic oracle gave the advice to "know thyself" thousands of years ago. Self-awareness means having a deep understanding of one's emotions, strengths, weaknesses, needs, and drives. People with strong self-aware-

The Five Components of Emotional Intelligence at Work

	Definition	Hallmarks
Self-Awareness	The ability to recognize and understand your moods, emotions, and drives, as well as their effect on others	Self-confidence Realistic self-assessment Self-deprecating sense of humor
Self-Regulation	The ability to control or redirect disruptive impulses and moods The propensity to suspend judgment—to think before acting	Trustworthiness and integrity Comfort with ambiguity Openness to change
Motivation	A passion to work for reasons that go beyond money or status A propensity to pursue goals with energy and persistence	Strong drive to achieve Optimism, even in the face of failure Organzational commitment
Empathy	The ability to understand the emotional makeup of other people Skill in treating people according to their emotional reactions	Expertise in building and retaining talent Cross-cultural sensitivity Service to clients and customers
Social Skill	Proficiency in managing relationships and building networks An ability to find common ground and build rapport	Effectiveness in leading change Persuasiveness Expertise in building and leading teams

ness are neither overly critical nor unrealistically hopeful. Rather, they are honest—with themselves and with others.

People who have a high degree of self-awareness recognize how their feelings affect them, other people, and their job performance. Thus a self-aware person who knows that tight deadlines bring out the worst in him plans his time carefully and gets his work done well in advance. Another person with high self-awareness will be able to work with a demanding client. She will understand the client's impact on her moods and the deeper reasons for her frustration. "Their trivial demands take us away from the real work that needs to be done," she might explain. And she will go one step further and turn her anger into something constructive.

Self-awareness extends to a person's understanding of his or her values and goals. Someone who is highly self-aware knows where he is headed and why; so, for example, he will be able to be firm in turning down a job offer that is tempting financially but does not fit with his principles or long-term goals. A person who lacks self-awareness is apt to make decisions that bring on inner turmoil by treading on buried values. "The money looked good so I signed on," someone might say two years into a job, "but the work means so little to me that I'm constantly bored." The decisions of self-aware people mesh with their values; consequently, they often find work to be energizing.

Self-aware job candidates will be frank in admitting to failure—and will often tell their tales with a smile.

How can one recognize self-awareness? First and foremost, it shows itself as candor and an ability to assess oneself realistically. People with high self-awareness are able to speak accurately and openly—although not necessarily effusively or confessionally—about their emotions and the impact they have on their work. For instance, one manager I know of was skeptical about a new personal-shopper service that her company, a major department-store chain, was about to introduce. Without prompting from her team or her boss, she offered them an explanation: "It's hard for me to get behind the rollout of this service," she admitted, "because I really wanted to run the project, but I wasn't selected. Bear with me while I deal with that." The manager did indeed examine her feelings; a week later, she was supporting the project fully.

Such self-knowledge often shows itself in the hiring process. Ask a candidate to describe a time he got carried away by his feelings and did something he later regretted. Self-aware candidates will be frank in admitting to failure—and will often tell their tales with a smile. One of the hallmarks of self-awareness is a self-deprecating sense of humor.

Self-awareness can also be identified during performance reviews. Self-aware people know—and are comfortable talking about—their limitations and strengths, and they often demonstrate a thirst for constructive criticism. By contrast, people with low self-awareness interpret the message that they need to improve as a threat or a sign of failure.

Self-aware people can also be recognized by their self-confidence. They have a firm grasp of their capabilities and are less likely to set themselves up to fail by, for example, overstretching on assignments. They know, too, when to ask for help. And the risks they take on the job are calculated. They won't ask for a challenge that they know they can't handle alone. They'll play to their strengths.

Consider the actions of a mid-level employee who was invited to sit in on a strategy meeting with her company's top executives. Although she was the most junior person in the room, she did not sit there quietly, listening in awestruck or fearful silence. She knew she had a head for clear logic and the skill to present ideas persuasively, and she offered cogent suggestions about the company's strategy. At the same time, her self-awareness stopped her from wandering into territory where she knew she was weak.

Despite the value of having self-aware people in the workplace, my research indicates that senior executives don't often give self-awareness the credit it deserves when they look for potential leaders. Many executives mistake candor about feelings for "wimpiness" and fail to give due respect to employees who openly acknowledge their shortcomings. Such people are too readily dismissed as "not tough enough" to lead others.

In fact, the opposite is true. In the first place, people generally admire and respect candor. Further, leaders are constantly required to make judgment calls that require a candid assessment of capabilities—their own and those of others. Do we have the management expertise to acquire a competitor? Can we launch a new product within six months? People who assess themselves honestly—that is, self-aware people—are well suited to do the same for the organizations they run.

Self-Regulation

Biological impulses drive our emotions. We cannot do away with them—but we can do much to manage them. Self-regulation, which is like an ongoing inner conversation, is the component of emotional intelligence that frees us from being prisoners of our feelings. People engaged in such a conversation feel bad moods and emotional impulses just as everyone else does, but they find ways to control them and even to channel them in useful ways.

Imagine an executive who has just watched a team of his employees present a botched analysis to the company's board of directors. In the gloom that follows, the executive might find himself tempted to pound on the table in anger or kick over a chair. He could leap up and scream at the group. Or he might maintain a grim silence, glaring at everyone before stalking off.

But if he had a gift for self-regulation, he would choose a different approach. He would pick his words carefully, acknowledging the team's poor performance without rushing to any hasty judgment. He would then step back to consider the reasons for the failure. Are they personal—a lack of effort? Are there any mitigating factors? What was his role in the debacle?

People who have mastered their emotions are able to roll with the changes. They don't panic.

After considering these questions, he would call the team together, lay out the incident's consequences, and offer his feelings about it. He would then present his analysis of the problem and a well-considered solution.

Why does self-regulation matter so much for leaders? First of all, people who are in control of their feelings and impulses—that is, people who are reasonable—are able to create an environment of trust and fairness. In such an environment, politics and infighting are sharply reduced and productivity is high. Talented people flock to the organization and aren't tempted to leave. And self-regulation has a trickle-down effect. No one wants to be known as a hothead when the boss is known for her calm approach. Fewer bad moods at the top mean fewer throughout the organization.

Second, self-regulation is important for competitive reasons. Everyone knows that business today is rife with ambiguity and change. Companies merge and break apart regularly. Technology transforms work at a dizzying pace. People who have mastered their emotions are able to roll with the changes. When a new change program is announced, they don't panic; instead, they are able to suspend judgment, seek out information, and listen to executives explain the new program. As the initiative moves forward, they are able to move with it.

Sometimes they even lead the way. Consider the case of a manager at a large manufacturing company. Like her colleagues, she had used a certain software program for five years. The program drove how she collected and reported data and how she thought about the company's strategy. One day, senior executives announced that a new program was to be installed that would radically change how information was gathered and assessed within the organization. While many people in the company complained bitterly about how disruptive the change would be, the manager mulled over the reasons for the new program and was convinced of its potential to improve performance. She eagerly attended training sessions—some of her colleagues refused to do so—and was eventually promoted to run several divisions, in part because she used the new technology so effectively.

I want to push the importance of self-regulation to leadership even further and make the case that it enhances integrity, which is not only a personal virtue but also an organizational strength. Many of the bad things that happen in companies are a function of impulsive behavior. People rarely plan to exaggerate profits, pad expense accounts, dip into the till, or abuse power for selfish ends. Instead, an opportunity presents itself, and people with low impulse control just say yes.

By contrast, consider the behavior of the senior executive at a large food company. The executive was scrupulously honest in his negotiations with local distributors. He would routinely lay out his cost structure in detail, thereby giving the distributors a realistic understanding of the company's pricing. This approach meant the executive couldn't always drive a hard bargain. Now, on occasion, he felt the urge to increase profits by withholding information about the company's costs. But he challenged that impulse—he saw that it made more sense in the long run to counteract it. His emotional self-regulation paid off in strong, lasting relationships with distributors that benefited the company more than any short-term financial gains would have.

The signs of emotional self-regulation, therefore, are not hard to miss: a propensity for reflection and thoughtfulness; comfort with ambiguity and change; and integrity—an ability to say no to impulsive urges.

Like self-awareness, self-regulation often does not get its due. People who can master their emotions are sometimes seen as cold fish—their considered responses are taken as a lack of passion. People with fiery temperaments are frequently thought of as "classic" leaders—their outbursts are considered hallmarks of charisma and power. But when such people make it to the top, their impulsiveness often works against them. In my research, extreme displays of negative emotion have never emerged as a driver of good leadership.

Motivation

If there is one trait that virtually all effective leaders have, it is motivation. They are driven to achieve beyond expectations—their own and everyone else's. The key word here is *achieve*. Plenty of people are motivated by external factors such as a big salary or the status that comes from having an impressive title or being part of a prestigious company. By contrast, those with leadership potential are motivated by a deeply embedded desire to achieve for the sake of achievement.

If you are looking for leaders, how can you identify people who are motivated by the drive to achieve rather than by external rewards? The first sign is a passion for the work itself—such people seek out creative challenges, love to learn, and take great pride in a job well done. They also display an unflagging energy to do things better. People with such energy often seem restless with the status quo. They are persistent with their questions about why things are done one way rather than another; they are eager to explore new approaches to their work.

A cosmetics company manager, for example, was frustrated that he had to wait two weeks to get sales results from people in the field. He finally tracked down an automated phone system that would beep each of his salespeople at 5 P.M. every day. An automated message then prompted them to punch in their numbers—how many calls and sales they had made that day. The system shortened the feedback time on sales results from weeks to hours.

That story illustrates two other common traits of people who are driven to achieve. They are forever raising the performance bar, and they like to keep score. Take the performance bar first. During performance reviews, people with high levels of motivation might ask to be "stretched" by their superiors. Of course, an employee who combines self-awareness with internal motivation will recognize her limits—but she won't settle for objectives that seem too easy to fulfill.

And it follows naturally that people who are driven to do better also want a way of tracking progress—their own, their team's, and their company's. Whereas people with low achievement motivation are often fuzzy about results, those with high achievement motivation often keep score by tracking such hard measures as profitability or market share. I know of a money manager who starts and ends his day on the Internet, gauging the performance of his stock fund against four industry-set benchmarks.

Interestingly, people with high motivation remain optimistic even when the score is against them. In such cases, self-regulation combines with achievement motivation to overcome the frustration and depression that come after a setback or failure. Take the case of another portfolio manager at a large investment company. After several successful years, her fund tumbled for three consecutive quarters, leading three large institutional clients to shift their business elsewhere.

Some executives would have blamed the nosedive on circumstances outside their control; others might have seen the setback as evidence of personal failure. This portfolio manager, however, saw an opportunity to prove she could lead a turnaround. Two years later, when she was promoted to a very senior level in the company, she described the experience as "the best thing that ever happened to me; I learned so much from it."

Executives trying to recognize high levels of achievement motivation in their people can look for one last piece of evidence: commitment to the organization. When people love their job for the work itself, they often feel committed to the organizations that make that work possible. Committed employees are likely to stay with an organization even when they are pursued by headhunters waving money.

The very word empathy *seems unbusinesslike, out of place amid the tough realities of the marketplace.*

It's not difficult to understand how and why a motivation to achieve translates into strong leadership. If you set the performance bar high for yourself, you will do the same for the organization when you are in a position to do so. Likewise, a drive to surpass goals and an interest in keeping score can be contagious. Leaders with these traits can often build a team of managers around them with the same traits. And of course, optimism and organizational commitment are fundamental to leadership—just try to imagine running a company without them.

Empathy

Of all the dimensions of emotional intelligence, empathy is the most easily recognized. We have all felt the empathy of a sensitive teacher or friend; we have all been struck by its absence in an unfeeling coach or boss. But when it comes to business, we rarely hear people praised, let alone rewarded, for their empathy. The very word seems unbusinesslike, out of place amid the tough realities of the marketplace.

But empathy doesn't mean a kind of "I'm okay, you're okay" mushiness. For a leader, that is, it doesn't mean adopting other people's emotions as one's own and trying to please everybody. That would be a nightmare—it would make action impossible. Rather, empathy means thoughtfully considering employees' feelings—along with other factors—in the process of making intelligent decisions.

For an example of empathy in action, consider what happened when two giant brokerage companies merged, creating redundant jobs in all their divisions. One division manager called his people together and gave a gloomy speech that emphasized the number of people who would soon be fired. The manager of another division gave his people a different kind of speech. He was upfront about his own worry and confusion, and he promised to keep people informed and to treat everyone fairly.

The difference between these two managers was empathy. The first manager was too worried about his own fate to consider the feelings of his anxiety-stricken colleagues. The second knew intuitively what his people were feeling, and he acknowledged their fears with his words. Is it any surprise that the first manager saw his division sink as many demoralized people, especially the most talented, departed? By contrast, the second manager continued to be a strong leader, his best people stayed, and his division remained as productive as ever.

Empathy is particularly important today as a component of leadership for at least three reasons: the increasing use of teams; the rapid pace of globalization; and the growing need to retain talent.

Consider the challenge of leading a team. As anyone who has ever been a part of one can attest, teams are cauldrons of bubbling emotions. They are often charged with reaching a consensus—hard enough with two people and much more difficult as the numbers increase. Even in groups with as few as four or five members, alliances form and clashing agendas get set. A team's leader must be able to sense and understand the viewpoints of everyone around the table.

That's exactly what a marketing manager at a large information technology company was able to do when she was appointed to lead a troubled team. The group was in turmoil, overloaded by work and missing deadlines. Tensions were high among the members. Tinkering with procedures was not enough to bring the group together and make it an effective part of the company.

So the manager took several steps. In a series of one-on-one sessions, she took the time to listen to everyone in the group—what was frustrating them, how they rated their colleagues, whether they felt they had been ignored. And then she directed the team in a way that brought it together: she encouraged people to speak more openly about their frustrations, and she helped people raise constructive complaints during meetings. In short, her empathy allowed her to understand her team's emotional makeup. The result was not just heightened collaboration among members but also added business, as the team was called on for help by a wider range of internal clients.

Globalization is another reason for the rising importance of empathy for business leaders. Cross-cultural dialogue can easily lead to miscues and misunderstandings. Empathy is an antidote. People who have it are attuned to subtleties in body language; they can hear the message beneath the words being spoken. Beyond that, they have a deep understanding of the existence and importance of cultural and ethnic differences.

Consider the case of an American consultant whose team had just pitched a project to a potential Japanese client. In its dealings with Americans, the team was accustomed to being bombarded with questions after such a proposal, but this time it was greeted with a long silence. Other members of the team, taking the silence as disapproval, were ready to pack and leave. The lead consultant gestured them to stop. Although he was not particularly familiar with Japanese culture, he read the client's face and posture and sensed not rejection but interest—even deep consideration. He was right: when the client finally spoke, it was to give the consulting firm the job.

Finally, empathy plays a key role in the retention of talent, particularly in today's information economy. Leaders have always needed empathy to develop and keep good people, but today the stakes are higher. When good people leave, they take the company's knowledge with them.

That's where coaching and mentoring come in. It has repeatedly been shown that coaching and mentoring pay off not just in better performance but also in increased job satisfaction and decreased turnover. But what makes coaching and mentoring work best is the nature of the relationship. Outstanding coaches and mentors get inside the heads of the people they are helping.

Social skill is friendliness with a purpose: moving people in the direction you desire.

They sense how to give effective feedback. They know when to push for better performance and when to hold back. In the way they motivate their protégés, they demonstrate empathy in action.

In what is probably sounding like a refrain, let me repeat that empathy doesn't get much respect in business. People wonder how leaders can make hard decisions if they are "feeling" for all the people who will be affected. But leaders with empathy do more than sympathize with people around them: they use their knowledge to improve their companies in subtle but important ways.

Social Skill

The first three components of emotional intelligence are all self-management skills. The last two, empathy and social skill, concern a person's ability to manage relationships with others. As a component of emotional intelligence, social skill is not as simple as it sounds. It's not just a matter of friendliness, although people with high levels of social skill are rarely mean-spirited. Social skill, rather, is friendliness with a purpose: moving people in the direction you desire, whether that's agreement on a new marketing strategy or enthusiasm about a new product.

Socially skilled people tend to have a wide circle of acquaintances, and they have a knack for finding common ground with people of all kinds—a knack for building rapport. That doesn't mean they socialize continually; it means they work according to the assumption that nothing important gets done alone. Such people have a network in place when the time for action comes.

Social skill is the culmination of the other dimensions of emotional intelligence. People tend to be very effective at managing relationships when they can understand and control their own emotions and can empathize with the feelings of others. Even motivation contributes to social skill. Remember that people who are driven to achieve tend to be optimistic, even in the face of setbacks or failure. When people are upbeat, their "glow" is cast upon conversations and other social encounters. They are popular, and for good reason.

Because it is the outcome of the other dimensions of emotional intelligence, social skill is recognizable on the job in many ways that will by now sound familiar. Socially skilled people, for instance, are adept at managing teams—that's their empathy at work. Likewise, they are expert persuaders—a manifestation of self-awareness, self-regulation, and empathy combined. Given those skills, good persuaders know when to make an emotional plea, for instance, and when an appeal to reason will work better. And motivation, when publicly visible, makes such people excellent collaborators; their passion for the work spreads to others, and they are driven to find solutions.

But sometimes social skill shows itself in ways the other emotional intelligence components do not. For instance, socially skilled people may at times appear not to be working while at work. They seem to be idly schmoozing—chatting in the hallways with colleagues or joking around with people who are not even connected to their "real" jobs. Socially skilled people, however, don't think it makes sense to arbitrarily limit the scope of their relationships. They build bonds widely because they know that in these fluid times, they may need help someday from people they are just getting to know today.

For example, consider the case of an executive in the strategy department of a global computer manufacturer. By 1993, he was convinced that the company's future lay with the Internet. Over the course of the next year, he found kindred spirits and used his social skill to stitch together a virtual community that cut across levels, divisions, and nations. He then used this de facto team to put up a corporate Web site, among the first by a major company. And, on his own initiative, with no budget or formal status, he signed up the company to participate in an annual Internet industry convention. Calling on his allies and persuading various divisions to donate funds, he recruited more than 50 people from a dozen different units to represent the company at the convention.

Management took notice: within a year of the conference, the executive's team formed the basis for the company's first Internet division, and he was formally put in charge of it. To get there, the executive had ignored conventional boundaries, forging and maintaining connections with people in every corner of the organization.

Is social skill considered a key leadership capability in most companies? The answer is yes, especially when compared with the other components of emotional intelligence. People seem to know intuitively that leaders need to manage relationships effectively; no leader is an island. After all, the leader's task is to get work done through other people, and social skill makes that possible. A leader who cannot express her empathy may as well not have it at all. And a leader's motivation will be useless if he cannot communicate his passion to the organization. Social skill allows leaders to put their emotional intelligence to work.

Emotional intelligence can be learned. The process is not easy. It takes time and commitment.

IT WOULD BE FOOLISH to assert that good-old-fashioned IQ and technical ability are not important ingredients in strong leadership. But the recipe would not be complete without emotional intelligence. It was once thought that the components of emotional intelligence were "nice to have" in business leaders. But now we know that, for the sake of performance, these are ingredients that leaders "need to have."

It is fortunate, then, that emotional intelligence can be learned. The process is not easy. It takes time and, most of all, commitment. But the benefits that come from having a well-developed emotional intelligence, both for the individual and for the organization, make it worth the effort.

Can Emotional Intelligence Be Learned?

FOR AGES, PEOPLE HAVE debated if leaders are born or made. So too goes the debate about emotional intelligence. Are people born with certain levels of empathy, for example, or do they acquire empathy as a result of life's experiences? The answer is both. Scientific inquiry strongly suggests that there is a genetic component to emotional intelligence. Psychological and developmental research indicates that nurture plays a role as well. How much of each perhaps will never be known, but research and practice clearly demonstrate that emotional intelligence can be learned.

One thing is certain: emotional intelligence increases with age. There is an old-fashioned word for the phenomenon: maturity. Yet even with maturity, some people still need training to enhance their emotional intelligence. Unfortunately, far too many training programs that intend to build leadership skills—including emotional intelligence—are a waste of time and money. The problem is simple: they focus on the wrong part of the brain.

Emotional intelligence is born largely in the neurotransmitters of the brain's limbic system, which governs feelings, impulses, and drives. Research indicates that the limbic system learns best through motivation, extended practice, and feedback. Compare this with the kind of learning that goes on in the neocortex, which governs analytical and technical ability. The neocortex grasps concepts and logic. It is the part of the brain that figures out how to use a computer or make a sales call by reading a book. Not surprisingly—but mistakenly—it is also the part of the brain targeted by most training programs aimed at enhancing emotional intelligence. When such programs take, in effect, a neocortical approach, my research with the Consortium for Research on Emotional Intelligence in Organizations has shown they can even have a *negative* impact on people's job performance.

To enhance emotional intelligence, organizations must refocus their training to include the limbic system. They must help people break old behavioral habits and establish new ones. That not only takes much more time than conventional training programs, it also requires an individualized approach.

Imagine an executive who is thought to be low on empathy by her colleagues. Part of that deficit shows itself as an inability to listen; she interrupts people and doesn't pay close attention to what they're saying. To fix the problem, the executive needs to be motivated to change, and then she needs practice and feedback from others in the company. A colleague or coach could be tapped to let the executive know when she has been observed failing to listen. She would then have to replay the incident and give a better response; that is, demonstrate her ability to absorb what others are saying. And the executive could be directed to observe certain executives who listen well and to mimic their behavior.

With persistence and practice, such a process can lead to lasting results. I know one Wall Street executive who sought to improve his empathy—specifically his ability to read people's reactions and see their perspectives. Before beginning his quest, the executive's subordinates were terrified of working with him. People even went so far as to hide bad news from him. Naturally, he was shocked when finally confronted with these facts. He went home and told his family—but they only confirmed what he had heard at work. When their opinions on any given subject did not mesh with his, they, too, were frightened of him.

Enlisting the help of a coach, the executive went to work to heighten his empathy through practice and feedback. His first step was to take a vacation to a foreign country where he did not speak the language. While there, he monitored his reactions to the unfamiliar and his openness to people who were different from him. When he returned home, humbled by his week abroad, the executive asked his coach to shadow him for parts of the day, several times a week, in order to critique how he treated people with new or different perspectives. At the same time, he consciously used on-the-job interactions as opportunities to practice "hearing" ideas that differed from his. Finally, the executive had himself videotaped in meetings and asked those who worked for and with him to critique his ability to acknowledge and understand the feelings of others. It took several months, but the executive's emotional intelligence did ultimately rise, and the improvement was reflected in his overall performance on the job.

It's important to emphasize that building one's emotional intelligence cannot—will not—happen without sincere desire and concerted effort. A brief seminar won't help; nor can one buy a how-to manual. It is much harder to learn to empathize—to internalize empathy as a natural response to people—than it is to become adept at regression analysis. But it can be done. "Nothing great was ever achieved without enthusiasm," wrote Ralph Waldo Emerson. If your goal is to become a real leader, these words can serve as a guidepost in your efforts to develop high emotional intelligence.

Originally published in November–December 1998
Reprint 98606

Narcissistic Leaders

The Incredible Pros,
the Inevitable Cons

MICHAEL MACCOBY

Executive Summary

TODAY'S BUSINESS LEADERS maintain a markedly higher profile than their predecessors did in the 1950s through the 1980s. Rather then hide behind the corporate veil, they give interviews to magazines like *Business Week, Time,* and the *Economist.* According to psychoanalyst, anthropologist, and consultant Michael Maccoby, this love of the limelight often stems from their personalities—in particular, what Freud called a narcissistic personality.

That is both good and bad news: Narcissists are good for companies that need people with vision and the courage to take them in new directions. But narcissists can also lead companies into trouble by refusing to listen to the advice and warnings of their managers.

So what can the narcissistic leader do to avoid the traps of his own personality? First, he can find a trusted

27

sidekick. Good sidekicks can point out the operational requirements of the narcissistic leader's often grandiose vision and keep him rooted in reality. Second, the narcissistic leader can get the people in his organization to identify with his goals, to think the way he does, and to become the living embodiment of the company. Finally, if narcissistic leaders can be persuaded to undergo therapy, they can use tools such as psychoanalysis to help overcome vital character flaws.

With the dramatic discontinuities going on in the world today, more and more larger corporations are finding there is no substitute for narcissistic leaders. For companies whose narcissistic leaders recognize their limits, these will be the best of times. For other companies, these could be the worst.

THERE'S SOMETHING NEW AND DARING about the CEOs who are transforming today's industries. Just compare them with the executives who ran large companies in the 1950s through the 1980s. Those executives shunned the press and had their comments carefully crafted by corporate PR departments. But today's CEOs—superstars such as Bill Gates, Andy Grove, Steve Jobs, Jeff Bezos, and Jack Welch—hire their own publicists, write books, grant spontaneous interviews, and actively promote their personal philosophies. Their faces adorn the covers of magazines like *Business Week*, *Time*, and the *Economist*. What's more, the world's business personalities are increasingly seen as the makers and shapers of our public and personal agendas. They advise schools on what kids should learn and lawmakers on how to invest the public's money. We look to them for thoughts on everything from the future of e-commerce to hot places to vacation.

There are many reasons today's business leaders have higher profiles than ever before. One is that business plays a much bigger role in our lives than it used to, and its leaders are more often in the limelight. Another is that the business world is experiencing enormous changes that call for visionary and charismatic leadership. But my 25 years of consulting both as a psychoanalyst in private practice and as an adviser to top managers suggest a third reason—namely, a pronounced change in the personality of the strategic leaders at the top. As an anthropologist, I try to understand people in the context in which they operate, and as a psychoanalyst, I tend to see them through a distinctly Freudian lens. Given what I know, I believe that the larger-than-life leaders we are seeing today closely resemble the personality type that Sigmund Freud dubbed narcissistic. "People of this type impress others as being 'personalities,' " he wrote, describing one of the psychological types that clearly fall within the range of normality. "They are especially suited to act as a support for others, to take on the role of leaders, and to give a fresh stimulus to cultural development or damage the established state of affairs."

Throughout history, narcissists have always emerged to inspire people and to shape the future. When military, religious, and political arenas dominated society, it was figures such as Napoléon Bonaparte, Mahatma Gandhi, and Franklin Delano Roosevelt who determined the social agenda. But from time to time, when business became the engine of social change, it, too, generated its share of narcissistic leaders. That was true at the beginning of this century, when men like Andrew Carnegie, John D. Rockefeller, Thomas Edison, and Henry Ford exploited new technologies and restructured American industry. And I think it is true again today.

But Freud recognized that there is a dark side to narcissism. Narcissists, he pointed out, are emotionally isolated and highly distrustful. Perceived threats can trigger rage. Achievements can feed feelings of grandiosity.

Productive narcissists have the audacity to push through the massive transformations that society periodically undertakes.

That's why Freud thought narcissists were the hardest personality types to analyze. Consider how an executive at Oracle describes his narcissistic CEO Larry Ellison: "The difference between God and Larry is that God does not believe he is Larry." That observation is amusing, but it is also troubling. Not surprisingly, most people think of narcissists in a primarily negative way. After all, Freud named the type after the mythical figure Narcissus, who died because of his pathological preoccupation with himself.

Yet narcissism can be extraordinarily useful—even necessary. Freud shifted his views about narcissism over time and recognized that we are all somewhat narcissistic. More recently, psychoanalyst Heinz Kohut built on Freud's theories and developed methods of treating narcissists. Of course, only professional clinicians are trained to tell if narcissism is normal or pathological. In this article, I discuss the differences between productive and unproductive narcissism but do not explore the extreme pathology of borderline conditions and psychosis.

Leaders such as Jack Welch and George Soros are examples of productive narcissists. They are gifted and creative strategists who see the big picture and find meaning in the risky challenge of changing the world and leaving behind a legacy. Indeed, one reason we look to productive narcissists in times of great transition is that they have the audacity to push through the massive transformations that society periodically undertakes. Productive narcissists are not only risk takers willing to get the job done but also charmers who can convert the masses with their rhetoric. The danger is that narcissism can turn unproductive when, lacking self-knowledge and restraining anchors, narcissists become unrealistic dreamers. They nurture grand schemes and harbor the illusion that only circumstances or enemies block their success. This tendency toward grandiosity and distrust is the Achilles' heel of narcissists. Because of it, even brilliant narcissists can come under suspicion for self-involvement, unpredictability, and—in extreme cases—paranoia.

It's easy to see why narcissistic leadership doesn't always mean successful leadership. Consider the case of Volvo's Pehr Gyllenhammar. He had a dream that appealed to a broad international audience—a plan to revolutionize the industrial workplace by replacing the dehumanizing assembly line caricatured in Charlie Chaplin's *Modern Times.* His wildly popular vision called for team-based craftsmanship. Model factories were built and publicized to international acclaim. But his success in pushing through these dramatic changes also sowed the seeds for his downfall. Gyllenhammar started to feel that he could ignore the concerns of his operational managers. He pursued chancy and expensive business deals, which he publicized on television and in the press. On one level, you can ascribe Gyllenhammar's falling out of touch with his workforce simply to faulty strategy. But it is also possible to attribute it to his narcissistic personality. His overestimation of himself led him to believe that others would want him to be the czar of a multinational enterprise. In turn, these fantasies led him to pursue a merger with Renault, which was tremendously unpopular with Swedish employees. Because Gyllenhammar was deaf to complaints about Renault, Swedish managers were forced to take their case public. In the end, shareholders aggressively rejected Gyllenhammar's plan, leaving him with no option but to resign.

Given the large number of narcissists at the helm of corporations today, the challenge facing organizations is to ensure that such leaders do not self-destruct or lead the company to disaster. That can take some doing because it is very hard for narcissists to work through their issues—and virtually impossible for them to do it alone. Narcissists need colleagues and even therapists if they hope to break free from their limitations. But because of their extreme independence and self-protectiveness, it is very difficult to get near them. Kohut maintained that a therapist would have to demonstrate an extraordinarily profound empathic understanding and sympathy for the narcissist's feelings in order to gain his trust. On top of that, narcissists must recognize that they can benefit from such help. For their part, employees must learn how to recognize—and work around—narcissistic bosses. To help them in this endeavor, let's first take a closer look at Freud's theory of personality types.

Three Main Personality Types

While Freud recognized that there are an almost infinite variety of personalities, he identified three main types: erotic, obsessive, and narcissistic. Most of us have elements of all three. We are all, for example, somewhat narcissistic. If that were not so, we would not be able to survive or assert our needs. The point is, one of the dynamic tendencies usually dominates the others, making each of us react differently to success and failure.

Freud's definitions of personality types differed over time. When talking about the erotic personality type, however, Freud generally did not mean a sexual personality but rather one for whom loving and above all being loved is most important. This type of individual is dependent on those people they fear will stop loving them. Many erotics are teachers, nurses, and social workers. At their most productive, they are developers of the young as well as enablers and helpers at work. As managers, they are caring and supportive, but they avoid conflict and make people dependent on them. They are, according to Freud, outer-directed people.

Obsessives, in contrast, are inner-directed. They are self-reliant and conscientious. They create and maintain order and make the most effective operational managers. They look constantly for ways to help people listen better, resolve conflict, and find win-win opportunities. They buy self-improvement books such as Stephen Covey's *The 7 Habits of Highly Effective People*. Obsessives are also ruled by a strict conscience—they like to focus on continuous improvement at work because it fits in with their sense of moral improvement. As entrepreneurs, obsessives start businesses that express their values, but they lack the vision, daring, and charisma it takes to turn a good idea into a great one. The best obsessives set high standards and communicate very effectively. They make sure that instructions are followed and costs are kept within budget. The most productive are great mentors and team players. The unproductive and the uncooperative become narrow experts and rule-bound bureaucrats.

Narcissists, the third type, are independent and not easily impressed. They are innovators, driven in business to gain power and glory. Productive narcissists are experts in their industries, but they go beyond it. They also pose the critical questions. They want to learn everything about everything that affects the company and its products. Unlike erotics, they want to be admired, not loved. And unlike obsessives, they are not troubled by a punishing superego, so they are able to aggressively pursue their goals. Of all the personality types, narcissists run the greatest risk of isolating themselves at the moment of success. And because of their independence and aggressiveness, they are constantly looking out for enemies, sometimes degenerating into paranoia when they are under extreme stress. (For more on personality types, see "Fromm's Fourth Personality Type" at the end of this article.)

Strengths of the Narcissistic Leader

When it comes to leadership, personality type can be instructive. Erotic personalities generally make poor managers—they need too much approval. Obsessives make better leaders—they are your operational managers: critical and cautious. But it is narcissists who come closest to our collective image of great leaders. There are two reasons for this: they have compelling, even gripping, visions for companies, and they have an ability to attract followers.

GREAT VISION

I once asked a group of managers to define a leader. "A person with vision" was a typical response. Productive narcissists understand the vision thing particularly well, because they are by nature people who see the big picture. They are not analyzers who can break up big questions into manageable problems; they aren't number crunchers either (these are usually the obsessives). Nor do they try to extrapolate to understand the future—they attempt to create it. To paraphrase George Bernard Shaw, some people see things as they are and ask why; narcissists see things that never were and ask why not.

Consider the difference between Bob Allen, a productive obsessive, and Mike Armstrong, a productive narcissist. In 1997, Allen tried to expand AT&T to reestablish the end-to-end service of the Bell System by reselling local service from the regional Bell operating companies (RBOCs). Although this was a worthwhile endeavor for shareholders and customers, it was hardly earth-shattering. By contrast, through a strategy of combining voice, telecommunications, and Internet access by high-speed broadband telecommunication over cable, Mike Armstrong has "created a new space with his name on it," as one of his colleagues puts it. Armstrong is betting that his costly strategy will beat out the RBOC's less expensive solution of digital subscriber lines over copper wire. This example illustrates the different approaches of obsessives and narcissists. The risk Armstrong took is one that few obsessives would feel comfortable taking. His vision is galvanizing AT&T. Who but a narcissistic leader could achieve such a thing? As Napoléon—a classic narcissist—once remarked, "Revolutions are ideal times for soldiers with a lot of wit—and the courage to act."

As in the days of the French Revolution, the world is now changing in astounding ways; narcissists have opportunities they would never have in ordinary times.

In short, today's narcissistic leaders have the chance to change the very rules of the game. Consider Robert B. Shapiro, CEO of Monsanto. Shapiro described his vision of genetically modifying crops as "the single most successful introduction of technology in the history of agriculture, including the plow" (*New York Times*, August 5, 1999). This is certainly a huge claim—there are still many questions about the safety and public acceptance of genetically engineered fruits and vegetables. But industries like agriculture are desperate for radical change. If Shapiro's gamble is successful, the industry will be transformed in the image of Monsanto. That's why he can get away with painting a picture of Monsanto as a highly profitable "life sciences" company—despite the fact that Monsanto's stock has fallen 12% from 1998 to the end of the third quarter of 1999. (During the same period, the S&P was up 41%.) Unlike Armstrong and Shapiro, it was enough for Bob Allen to win against his competitors in a game measured primarily by the stock market. But narcissistic leaders are after something more. They want—and need—to leave behind a legacy.

SCORES OF FOLLOWERS

Narcissists have vision—but that's not enough. People in mental hospitals also have visions. The simplest definition of a leader is someone whom other people follow. Indeed, narcissists are especially gifted in attracting followers, and more often than not, they do so through language. Narcissists believe that words can move mountains and that inspiring speeches can change people. Narcissistic leaders are often skillful orators, and this is one of the talents that makes them so charismatic.

Indeed, anyone who has seen narcissists perform can attest to their personal magnetism and their ability to stir enthusiasm among audiences.

Yet this charismatic gift is more of a two-way affair than most people think. Although it is not always obvious, narcissistic leaders are quite dependent on their followers—they need affirmation, and preferably adulation. Think of Winston Churchill's wartime broadcasts or J.F.K.'s "Ask not what your country can do for you" inaugural address. The adulation that follows from such speeches bolsters the self-confidence and conviction of the speakers. But if no one responds, the narcissist usually becomes insecure, overly shrill, and insistent—just as Ross Perot did.

Even when people respond positively to a narcissist, there are dangers. That's because charisma is a double-edged sword—it fosters both closeness and isolation. As he becomes increasingly self-assured, the narcissist becomes more spontaneous. He feels free of constraints. Ideas flow. He thinks he's invincible. This energy and confidence further inspire his followers. But the very

One of his greatest problems is that the narcissist's faults tend to become even more pronounced as he becomes more successful.

adulation that the narcissist demands can have a corrosive effect. As he expands, he listens even less to words of caution and advice. After all, he has been right before, when others had their doubts. Rather than try to persuade those who disagree with him, he feels justified in ignoring them—creating further isolation. The result is sometimes flagrant risk taking that can lead to catastrophe. In the political realm, there is no clearer example of this than Bill Clinton.

Weaknesses of the Narcissistic Leader

Despite the warm feelings their charisma can evoke, narcissists are typically not comfortable with their own
emotions. They listen only for the kind of information
they seek. They don't learn easily from others. They don't
like to teach but prefer to indoctrinate and make
speeches. They dominate meetings with subordinates.
The result for the organization is greater internal competitiveness at a time when everyone is already under as
much pressure as they can possibly stand. Perhaps the
main problem is that the narcissist's faults tend to
become even more pronounced as he becomes more
successful.

SENSITIVE TO CRITICISM

Because they are extraordinarily sensitive, narcissistic
leaders shun emotions as a whole. Indeed, perhaps one of
the greatest paradoxes in this age of teamwork and part-
nering is that the best corporate leader in the contemporary world is the type of person who is emotionally isolated. Narcissistic leaders typically keep others at arm's
length. They can put up a wall of defense as thick as the
Pentagon. And given their difficulty with knowing or
acknowledging their own feelings, they are uncomfortable with other people expressing theirs—especially their
negative feelings.

Indeed, even productive narcissists are extremely sensitive to criticism or slights, which feel to them like
knives threatening their self-image and their confidence
in their visions. Narcissists are almost unimaginably
thin-skinned. Like the fairy-tale princess who slept on

many mattresses and yet knew she was sleeping on a pea, narcissists—even powerful CEOs—bruise easily. This is one explanation why narcissistic leaders do not want to know what people think of them unless it is causing them a real problem. They cannot tolerate dissent. In fact, they can be extremely abrasive with employees who doubt them or with subordinates who are tough enough to fight back. Steve Jobs, for example, publicly humiliates subordinates. Thus, although narcissistic leaders often say that they want teamwork, what that means in practice is that they want a group of yes-men. As the more independent-minded players leave or are pushed out, succession becomes a particular problem.

POOR LISTENERS

One serious consequence of this oversensitivity to criticism is that narcissistic leaders often do not listen when they feel threatened or attacked. Consider the response of one narcissistic CEO I had worked with for three years who asked me to interview his immediate team and report back to him on what they were thinking. He invited me to his summer home to discuss what I had found. "So what do they think of me?" he asked with seeming nonchalance. "They think you are very creative and courageous," I told him, "but they also feel that you don't listen." "Excuse me, what did you say?" he shot back at once, pretending not to hear. His response was humorous, but it was also tragic. In a very real way, this CEO could not hear my criticism because it was too painful to tolerate. Some narcissists are so defensive that they go so far as to make a virtue of the fact that they don't listen. As another CEO bluntly put it, "I didn't get here by listening to people!" Indeed, on one occasion when this CEO proposed a daring strategy, none of his subordinates believed it would work. His subsequent success strengthened his conviction that he had nothing to learn about strategy from his lieutenants. But success is no excuse for narcissistic leaders not to listen.

LACK OF EMPATHY

Best-selling business writers today have taken up the slogan of "emotional competencies"—the belief that successful leadership requires a strongly developed sense of empathy. But although they crave empathy from others, productive narcissists are not noted for being particularly empathetic themselves. Indeed, lack of empathy is a characteristic shortcoming of some of the most charismatic and successful narcissists, including Bill Gates and Andy Grove. Of course, leaders do need to communicate persuasively. But a lack of empathy did not prevent some of history's greatest narcissistic leaders from knowing how to communicate—and inspire. Neither Churchill, de Gaulle, Stalin, nor Mao Tse-tung were empathetic. And yet they inspired people because of their passion and their conviction at a time when people longed for certainty. In fact, in times of radical change, lack of empathy can actually be a strength. A narcissist finds it easier than other personality types to buy and sell companies, to close and move facilities, and to lay off employees—decisions that inevitably make many people angry and sad. But narcissistic leaders typically have few regrets. As one

There is a kind of emotional intelligence associated with narcissists, but it's more street smarts than empathy.

CEO says," If I listened to my employees' needs and demands, they would eat me alive."

Given this lack of empathy, it's hardly surprising that narcissistic leaders don't score particularly well on evaluations of their interpersonal style. What's more, neither 360-degree evaluations of their management style nor workshops in listening will make them more empathic. Narcissists don't want to change—and as long as they are successful, they don't think they have to. They may see the need for operational managers to get touchy-feely training, but that's not for them.

There is a kind of emotional intelligence associated with narcissists, but it's more street smarts than empathy. Narcissistic leaders are acutely aware of whether or not people are with them wholeheartedly. They know whom they can use. They can be brutally exploitative. That's why, even though narcissists undoubtedly have "star quality," they are often unlikable. They easily stir up people against them, and it is only in tumultuous times, when their gifts are desperately needed, that people are willing to tolerate narcissists as leaders.

DISTASTE FOR MENTORING

Lack of empathy and extreme independence make it difficult for narcissists to mentor and be mentored. Generally speaking, narcissistic leaders set very little store by mentoring. They seldom mentor others, and when they do they typically want their protégés to be pale reflections of themselves. Even those narcissists like Jack Welch who are held up as strong mentors are usually more interested in instructing than in coaching.

Narcissists certainly don't credit mentoring or educational programs for their own development as leaders. A few narcissistic leaders such as Bill Gates may find a friend or consultant—for instance, Warren Buffet, a superproductive obsessive—whom they can trust to be their guide and confidant. But most narcissists prefer "mentors" they can control. A 32-year-old marketing vice president, a narcissist with CEO potential, told me that she had rejected her boss as a mentor. As she put it, "First of all, I want to keep the relationship at a distance. I don't want to be influenced by emotions. Second, there are things I don't want him to know. I'd rather hire an outside consultant to be my coach." Although narcissistic leaders appear to be at ease with others, they find intimacy—which is a prerequisite for mentoring—to be difficult. Younger narcissists will establish peer relations with authority rather than seek a parentlike mentoring relationship. They want results and are willing to take chances arguing with authority.

AN INTENSE DESIRE TO COMPETE

Narcissistic leaders are relentless and ruthless in their pursuit of victory. Games are not games but tests of their survival skills. Of course, all successful managers want to win, but narcissists are not restrained by conscience. Organizations led by narcissists are generally characterized by intense internal competition. Their passion to win is marked by both the promise of glory and the primitive danger of extinction. It is a potent brew that energizes companies, creating a sense of urgency, but it can also be dangerous. These leaders see everything as a threat. As Andy Grove puts it, brilliantly articulating the narcissist's fear, distrust, and aggression, "Only the paranoid survive." The concern, of course, is that the narcissist finds enemies that aren't there—even among his colleagues.

Avoiding the Traps

There is very little business literature that tells narcissistic leaders how to avoid the pitfalls. There are two reasons for this. First, relatively few narcissistic leaders are interested in looking inward. And second, psychoanalysts don't usually get close enough to them, especially in the workplace, to write about them. (The noted psychoanalyst Harry Levinson is an exception.) As a result, advice on leadership focuses on obsessives, which explains why so much of it is about creating teamwork and being more receptive to subordinates. But as we've already seen, this literature is of little interest to narcissists, nor is it likely to help subordinates understand their narcissistic leaders. The absence of managerial literature on narcissistic leaders doesn't mean that it is impossible to devise strategies for dealing with narcissism. In the course of a long career counseling CEOs, I have identified three basic ways in which productive narcissists can avoid the traps of their own personality.

FIND A TRUSTED SIDEKICK

Many narcissists can develop a close relationship with one person, a sidekick who acts as an anchor, keeping the narcissistic partner grounded. However, given that narcissistic leaders trust only their own insights and view of reality, the sidekick has to understand the narcissistic leader and what he is trying to achieve. The narcissist must feel that this person, or in some cases persons, is practically an extension of himself. The side-kick must also be sensitive enough to manage the relationship. Don Quixote is a classic example of a narcissist who was out of touch with reality but who was constantly saved from disaster by his squire Sancho Panza. Not surprisingly, many narcissistic leaders rely heavily on their spouses, the people they are closest to. But dependence on spouses can be risky, because they may further isolate the narcissistic leader from his company by supporting his grandiosity and feeding his paranoia. I once knew a CEO in this kind of relationship with his spouse. He took to accusing loyal subordinates of plotting against him just because they ventured a few criticisms of his ideas.

It is much better for a narcissistic leader to choose a colleague as his sidekick. Good sidekicks are able to point out the operational requirements of the narcissistic leader's vision and keep him rooted in reality. The best sidekicks are usually productive obsessives. Gyllenhammar, for instance, was most effective at Volvo when he had an obsessive COO, Håkan Frisinger, to focus on improving quality and cost, as well as an obsessive HR director, Berth Jönsson, to implement his vision. Similarly, Bill Gates can think about the future from the stratosphere because Steve Ballmer, a tough obsessive president, keeps the show on the road. At Oracle, CEO Larry Ellison can afford to miss key meetings and spend time on his boat contemplating a future without PCs because he has a productive obsessive COO in Ray Lane to run the company for him. But the job of sidekick entails more than just executing the leader's ideas. The sidekick also has to get his leader to accept new ideas. To do this, he must be able to show the leader how the new ideas fit with his views and serve his interests. (For more on dealing with narcissistic bosses, see "Working for a Narcissist" at the end of this article.)

INDOCTRINATE THE ORGANIZATION

The narcissistic CEO wants all his subordinates to think the way he does about the business. Productive narcissists—people who often have a dash of the obsessive personality—are good at converting people to their point of view. One of the most successful at this is GE's Jack Welch. Welch uses toughness to build a corporate culture and to implement a daring business strategy, including the buying and selling of scores of companies. Unlike other narcissistic leaders such as Gates, Grove, and Ellison, who have transformed industries with new products, Welch was able to transform his industry by focusing on execution and pushing companies to the limits of quality and efficiency, bumping up revenues and wringing out costs. In order to do so, Welch hammers out a huge corporate culture in his own image—a culture that provides impressive rewards for senior managers and shareholders.

Welch's approach to culture building is widely misunderstood. Many observers, notably Noel Tichy in *The Leadership Engine*, argue that Welch forms his company's leadership culture through teaching. But Welch's "teaching" involves a personal ideology that he indoctrinates into GE managers through speeches, memos, and confrontations. Rather than create a dialogue, Welch makes pronouncements (either be the number one or two company in your market or get out), and he institutes programs (such as Six Sigma quality) that become the GE party line. Welch's strategy has been extremely effective. GE managers must either internalize his vision, or they must leave. Clearly, this is incentive learning with a vengeance. I would even go so far as to call Welch's teaching brainwashing. But Welch does have the rare insight and know-how to achieve what all narcissistic business leaders are trying to do—namely, get the organization to identify with them, to think the way they do, and to become the living embodiment of their companies.

GET INTO ANALYSIS

Narcissists are often more interested in controlling others than in knowing and disciplining themselves. That's why, with very few exceptions, even productive narcissists do not want to explore their personalities with the help of insight therapies such as psychoanalysis. Yet since Heinz Kohut, there has been a radical shift in psychoanalytic thinking about what can be done to help narcissists work through their rage, alienation, and grandiosity. Indeed, if they can be persuaded to undergo therapy, narcissistic leaders can use tools such as psychoanalysis to overcome vital character flaws.

Consider the case of one exceptional narcissistic CEO who asked me to help him understand why he so often lost his temper with subordinates. He lived far from my home city, and so the therapy was sporadic and very unorthodox. Yet he kept a journal of his dreams, which we interpreted together either by phone or when we met. Our analysis uncovered painful feelings of being unappreciated that went back to his inability to impress a cold father. He came to realize that he demanded an unreasonable amount of praise and that when he felt unappreciated by his subordinates, he became furious. Once he understood that, he was able to recognize his narcissism and even laugh about it. In the middle of our work, he even announced to his top team that I was psychoanalyzing him and asked them what they thought of that. After a pregnant pause, one executive vice president piped up, "Whatever you're doing, you should keep doing it, because you don't get so angry anymore." Instead of being trapped by narcissistic rage, this CEO was learning how to express his concerns constructively.

Leaders who can work on themselves in that way tend to be the most productive narcissists. In addition to being self-reflective, they are also likely to be open, likable, and good-humored. Productive narcissists have perspective; they are able to detach themselves and laugh at their irrational needs. Although serious about achieving their goals, they are also playful. As leaders, they are aware of being performers. A sense of humor helps them maintain enough perspective and humility to keep on learning.

The Best and Worst of Times

As I have pointed out, narcissists thrive in chaotic times. In more tranquil times and places, however, even the most brilliant narcissist will seem out of place. In his short story *The Curfew Tolls*, Stephen Vincent Benét speculates on what would have happened to Napoléon if he had been born some 30 years earlier. Retired in prerevolutionary France, Napoléon is depicted as a lonely artillery major boasting to a vacationing British general about how he could have beaten the English in India. The point, of course, is that a visionary born in the wrong time can seem like a pompous buffoon.

Historically, narcissists in large corporations have been confined to sales positions, where they use their persuasiveness and imagination to best effect. In settled times, the problematic side of the narcissistic personality usually conspires to keep narcissists in their place, and they can typically rise to top management positions only by starting their own companies or by leaving to lead upstarts. Consider Joe Nacchio, formerly in charge of both the business and consumer divisions of AT&T. Nacchio was a super-salesman and a popular leader in the mid-1990s. But his desire to create a new network for business customers was thwarted by colleagues who found him abrasive, self-promoting, and ruthlessly ambitious.

More and more corporations are finding there is no substitute for narcissistic leaders in this age of innovation.

Two years ago, Nacchio left AT&T to become CEO of Qwest, a company that is creating a long-distance fiber-optic cable network. Nacchio had the credibility—and charisma—to sell Qwest's initial public offering to financial markets and gain a high valuation. Within a short space of time, he turned Qwest into an attractive target for the RBOCs, which were looking to move into long-distance telephony and Internet services. Such a sale would have given Qwest's owners a handsome profit on their investment. But Nacchio wanted more. He wanted to expand—to compete with AT&T—and for that he needed local service. Rather than sell Qwest, he chose to make a bid himself for local telephone operator U.S. West, using Qwest's highly valued stock to finance the deal. The market voted on this display of expansiveness with its feet—Qwest's stock price fell 40% between last June, when he made the deal, and the end of the third quarter of 1999. (The S&P index dropped 5.7% during the same period.)

Like other narcissists, Nacchio likes risk—and sometimes ignores the costs. But with the dramatic discontinuities going on in the world today, more and more large corporations are getting into bed with narcissists. They are finding that there is no substitute for narcissistic leaders in an age of innovation. Companies need leaders who do not try to anticipate the future so much as create it. But narcissistic leaders—even the most productive of them—can self-destruct and lead their organizations terribly astray. For companies whose narcissistic leaders recognize their limitations, these will be the best of times. For other companies, these could turn out to be the worst.

Fromm's Fourth Personality Type

NOT LONG AFTER FREUD described his three personality types in 1931, psychoanalyst Erich Fromm proposed a fourth personality type, which has become particularly prevalent in today's service economy. Fromm called this type the "marketing personality," and it is exemplified by the lead character in Woody Allen's movie *Zelig*, a man so governed by his need to be valued that he becomes exactly like the people he happens to be around.

Marketing personalities are more detached than erotics and so are less likely to cement close ties. They are also less driven by conscience than obsessives. Instead, they are motivated by a radarlike anxiety that permeates everything they do. Because they are so eager to please and to alleviate this anxiety, marketing personalities excel at selling themselves to others.

Unproductive marketing types lack direction and the ability to commit themselves to people or projects. But when productive, marketing types are good at facilitating teams and keeping the focus on adding value as defined by customers and colleagues. Like obsessives, marketing personalities are avid consumers of self-help books. Like narcissists, they are not wedded to the past. But marketing types generally make poor leaders in times of crisis. They lack the daring needed to innovate and are too responsive to current, rather than future, customer demands.

The Rise and Fall of a Narcissist

THE STORY OF JAN CARLZON, the former CEO of the Scandinavian airline SAS, is an almost textbook example of how a narcissist's weaknesses can cut short a brilliant career. In the 1980s, Carlzon's vision of SAS as the businessperson's airline was widely acclaimed in the business press; management guru Tom Peters described him as a model leader. In 1989, when I first met Carlzon and his management team, he compared the ideal organization to the Brazilian soccer team—in principle, there would be no fixed roles, only innovative plays. I asked the members of the management team if they agreed with this vision of an empowered front line. One vice president, a former pilot, answered no. "I still believe that the best organization is the military," he said. I then asked Carlzon for his reaction to that remark. "Well," he replied, "that may be true, if your goal is to shoot your customers."

That rejoinder was both witty and dismissive; clearly, Carlzon was not engaging in a serious dialogue with his subordinates. Nor was he listening to other advisers.

Carlzon ignored the issue of high costs, even when many observers pointed out that SAS could not compete without improving productivity. He threw money at expensive acquisitions of hotels and made an unnecessary investment in Continental Airlines just months before it declared bankruptcy.

Carlzon's story perfectly corroborates the often-recorded tendency of narcissists to become overly expansive—and hence isolated—at the very pinnacle of their success. Seduced by the flattery he received in the international press, Carlzon's self-image became so enormously inflated that his feet left the ground. And given his vulnerability to grandiosity, he was propelled by a need to expand his organization rather than develop it. In due course, as Carlzon led the company deeper and deeper into losses, he was fired. Now he is a venture capitalist helping budding companies. And SAS has lost its glitter.

Working for a Narcissist

DEALING WITH A narcissistic boss isn't easy. You have to be prepared to look for another job if your boss becomes too narcissistic to let you disagree with him. But remember that the company is typically betting on *his* vision of the future—not yours. Here are a few tips on how to survive in the short term:

- Always empathize with your boss's feelings, but don't expect any empathy back. Look elsewhere for your own self-esteem. Understand that behind his display of infallibility, there hides a deep vulnerability. Praise his achievements and reinforce his best impulses, but don't be shamelessly sycophantic. An intelligent narcissist can see through flatterers and prefers independent people who truly appreciate him. Show that you will protect his image, inside and outside the company. But be careful if he asks for an honest evaluation. What he wants is information that will help him solve a problem about his image. He will resent any honesty that threatens his inflated self-image and will likely retaliate.

- Give your boss ideas, but always let him take the credit for them. Find out what he thinks before presenting your views. If you believe he is wrong, show how a different approach would be in his best interest. Take his paranoid views seriously, don't brush them aside—they often reveal sharp intuitions. Disagree only when you can demonstrate how he will benefit from a different point of view.

- Hone your time-management skills. Narcissistic leaders often give subordinates many more orders than they can possibly execute. Ignore the requests he makes that don't make sense. Forget about them. He will. But be careful: carve out free time for yourself only when you know there's a lull in the boss's schedule. Narcissistic leaders feel free to call you at any hour of the day or night. Make yourself available, or be prepared to get out.

Originally published in January–February 2000
Reprint R00105

Leadership That Gets Results

DANIEL GOLEMAN

Executive Summary

A LEADER'S SINGULAR JOB is to get results. But even
with all the leadership training programs and "expert"
advice available, effective leadership still eludes many
people and organizations. One reason, says Daniel
Goleman, is that such experts offer advice based on
inference, experience, and instinct, not on quantitative
data.

Now, drawing on research of more then 3,000 executives, Goleman explores which precise leadership
behaviors yield positive results. He outlines six distinct
leadership styles, each one springing from different components of emotional intelligence. Each style has a distinct effect on the working atmosphere of a company,
division, or team, and in turn, on its financial performance. The styles, by name and brief description alone,
will resonate with anyone who leads, is led, or, as is the

53

case with most of us, does both. *Coercive leaders* demand immediate compliance *Authoritative leaders* mobilize people toward a vision. *Affiliative leaders* create emotional bonds and harmony. *Democratic leaders* build consensus through participation. *Pacesetting leaders* expect excellence and self-direction. And *coaching leaders* develop people for the future.

The research indicates that leaders who get the best results don't rely on just one leadership style; they use most of the styles in any given week. Goleman details the types of business situations each style is best suited for, and he explains how leaders who lack one or more of these styles can expand their repertoires. He maintains that with practice leaders can switch among leadership styles to produce powerful results, thus turning the art of leadership into a science.

A SK ANY GROUP of businesspeople the question "What do effective leaders do?" and you'll hear a sweep of answers. Leaders set strategy; they motivate; they create a mission; they build a culture. Then ask "What *should* leaders do?" If the group is seasoned, you'll likely hear one response: the leader's singular job is to get results.

But how? The mystery of what leaders can and ought to do in order to spark the best performance from their people is age-old. In recent years, that mystery has spawned an entire cottage industry: literally thousands of "leadership experts" have made careers of testing and coaching executives, all in pursuit of creating businesspeople who can turn bold objectives—be they strategic, financial, organizational, or all three—into reality.

Still, effective leadership eludes many people and organizations. One reason is that until recently, virtually no quantitative research has demonstrated which precise leadership behaviors yield positive results. Leadership experts proffer advice based on inference, experience, and instinct. Sometimes that advice is right on target; sometimes it's not.

But new research by the consulting firm Hay/McBer, which draws on a random sample of 3,871 executives selected from a database of more than 20,000 executives worldwide, takes much of the mystery out of effective leadership. The research found six distinct leadership styles, each springing from different components of emotional intelligence. The styles, taken individually, appear to have a direct and unique impact on the working atmosphere of a company, division, or team, and in turn, on its financial performance. And perhaps most important, the research indicates that leaders with the best results do not rely on only one leadership style; they use most of them in a given week—seamlessly and in different measure—depending on the business situation. Imagine the styles, then, as the array of clubs in a golf pro's bag. Over the course of a game, the pro picks and chooses clubs based on the demands of the shot. Sometimes he has to ponder his selection, but usually it is automatic. The pro senses the challenge ahead, swiftly pulls out the right tool, and elegantly puts it to work. That's how high-impact leaders operate, too.

What are the six styles of leadership? None will shock workplace veterans. Indeed, each style, by name and brief description alone, will likely resonate with anyone who leads, is led, or as is the case with most of us, does both. *Coercive leaders* demand immediate compliance. *Authoritative leaders* mobilize people toward a vision.

Affiliative leaders create emotional bonds and harmony. *Democratic leaders* build consensus through participation. *Pacesetting leaders* expect excellence and self-direction. And *coaching leaders* develop people for the future.

Close your eyes and you can surely imagine a colleague who uses any one of these styles. You most likely use at least one yourself. What is new in this research, then, is its implications for action. First, it offers a fine-grained understanding of how different leadership styles affect performance and results. Second, it offers clear guidance on when a manager should switch between them. It also strongly suggests that switching flexibly is well advised. New, too, is the research's finding that each leadership style springs from different components of emotional intelligence.

Measuring Leadership's Impact

It has been more than a decade since research first linked aspects of emotional intelligence to business results. The late David McClelland, a noted Harvard University psychologist, found that leaders with strengths in a critical mass of six or more emotional intelligence competencies were far more effective than peers who lacked such strengths. For instance, when he analyzed the performance of division heads at a global food and beverage company, he found that among leaders with this critical mass of competence, 87% placed in the top third for annual salary bonuses based on their business performance. More telling, their divisions on average outperformed yearly revenue targets by 15% to 20%. Those executives who lacked emotional intelligence were rarely rated as outstanding in their annual performance reviews, and their divisions underperformed by an average of almost 20%.

Our research set out to gain a more molecular view of the links among leadership and emotional intelligence, and climate and performance. A team of McClelland's colleagues headed by Mary Fontaine and Ruth Jacobs from Hay/McBer studied data about or observed thousands of executives, noting specific behaviors and their impact on climate.[1] How did each individual motivate direct reports? Manage change initiatives? Handle crises? It was in a later phase of the research that we identified which emotional intelligence capabilities drive the six leadership styles. How does he rate in terms of self-control and social skill? Does a leader show high or low levels of empathy?

The team tested each executive's immediate sphere of influence for its climate. "Climate" is not an amorphous term. First defined by psychologists George Litwin and Richard Stringer and later refined by McClelland and his colleagues, it refers to six key factors that influence an organization's working environment: its *flexibility*—that is, how free employees feel to innovate unencumbered by red tape; their sense of *responsibility* to the organization; the level of *standards* that people set; the sense of accuracy about performance feedback and aptness of *rewards*; the *clarity* people have about mission and values; and finally, the level of *commitment* to a common purpose.

We found that all six leadership styles have a measurable effect on each aspect of climate. (For details, see the exhibit "Getting Molecular: The Impact of Leadership Styles on Drivers of Climate.") Further, when we looked at the impact of climate on financial results—such as return on sales, revenue growth, efficiency, and profitability—we found a direct correlation between the two. Leaders who used styles that positively affected the climate had decidedly better financial results than those who did not. That is not to say that organizational

Getting Molecular:

The Impact of Leadership Styles on Drivers of Climate

Our research investigated how each leadership style affected the six drivers of climate, or working atmosphere. The figures below show the correlation between each leadership style and each aspect of climate. So, for instance, if we look at the climate driver of flexibility, we see that the coercive style has a -.28 correlation while the democratic style has a .28 correlation, equally strong in the opposite direction. Focusing on the authoritative leadership style, we find that it has a .54 correlation with rewards—strongly positive—and a .21 correlation with responsibility—positive, but not as strong. In other words, the style's correlation with rewards was more than twice that with responsibility.

According to the data, the authoritative leadership style has the most positive effect on climate, but three others—affiliative, democratic, and coaching—follow close behind. That said, the research indicates that no style should be relied on exclusively, and all have at least short-term uses.

	Coercive	Authoritative	Affiliative	Democratic	Pacesetting	Coaching
Flexibility	-.28	.32	.27	.28	-.07	.17
Responsibility	-.37	.21	.16	.23	.04	.08
Standards	.02	.38	.31	.22	-.27	.39
Rewards	-.18	.54	.48	.42	-.29	.43
Clarity	-.11	.44	.37	.35	-.28	.38
Commitment	-.13	.35	.34	.26	-.20	.27
Overall impact on climate	-.26	.54	.46	.43	-.25	.42

climate is the only driver of performance. Economic conditions and competitive dynamics matter enormously. But our analysis strongly suggests that climate accounts for nearly a third of results. And that's simply too much of an impact to ignore.

The Styles in Detail

Executives use six leadership styles, but only four of the six consistently have a positive effect on climate and results. Let's look then at each style of leadership in detail. (For a summary of the material that follows, see the chart "The Six Leadership Styles at a Glance.")

THE COERCIVE STYLE

The computer company was in crisis mode—its sales and profits were falling, its stock was losing value precipitously, and its shareholders were in an uproar. The board brought in a new CEO with a reputation as a turnaround artist. He set to work chopping jobs, selling off divisions, and making the tough decisions that should have been executed years before. The company was saved, at least in the short-term.

From the start, though, the CEO created a reign of terror, bullying and demeaning his executives, roaring his displeasure at the slightest misstep. The company's top echelons were decimated not just by his erratic firings but also by defections. The CEO's direct reports, frightened by his tendency to blame the bearer of bad news, stopped bringing him any news at all. Morale was at an all-time low—a fact reflected in another downturn in the business after the short-term recovery. The CEO was eventually fired by the board of directors.

The Six Leadership Styles at a Glance

Our research found that leaders use six styles, each springing from different components of emotional intelligence. Here is a summary of the styles, their origin, when they work best, and their impact on an organization's climate and thus its performance.

	Coercive	Authoritative	Affiliative	Democratic	Pacesetting	Coaching
The leader's modus operandi	Demands immediate compliance	Mobilizes people toward a vision	Creates harmony and builds emotional bonds	Forges consensus through participation	Sets high standards for performance	Develops people for the future
The style in a phrase	"Do what I tell you."	"Come with me."	"People come first."	"What do you think?"	"Do as I do, now."	"Try this."
Underlying emotional intelligence competencies	Drive to achieve, initiative, self-control	Self-confidence, empathy, change catalyst	Empathy, building relationships, communication	Collaboration, team leadership, communication	Conscientiousness, drive to achieve, initiative	Developing others, empathy, self-awareness
When the style works best	In a crisis, to kick start a turnaround, or with problem employees	When changes require a new vision, or when a clear direction is needed	To heal rifts in a team or to motivate people during stressful circumstances	To build buy-in or consensus, or to get input from valuable employees	To get quick results from a highly motivated and competent team	To help an employee improve performance or develop long-term strengths
Overall impact on climate	Negative	Most strongly positive	Positive	Positive	Negative	Positive

It's easy to understand why of all the leadership styles, the coercive one is the least effective in most situations. Consider what the style does to an organization's climate. Flexibility is the hardest hit. The leader's extreme top-down decision making kills new ideas on the vine. People feel so disrespected that they think, "I won't even bring my ideas up—they'll only be shot down." Likewise, people's sense of responsibility evaporates: unable to act on their own initiative, they lose their sense of ownership and feel little accountability for their performance. Some become so resentful they adopt the attitude, "I'm not going to help this bastard."

Coercive leadership also has a damaging effect on the rewards system. Most high-performing workers are motivated by more than money—they seek the satisfaction of work well done. The coercive style erodes such pride. And finally, the style undermines one of the leader's prime tools—motivating people by showing them how their job fits into a grand, shared mission. Such a loss, measured in terms of diminished clarity and commitment, leaves people alienated from their own jobs, wondering, "How does any of this matter?"

Given the impact of the coercive style, you might assume it should never be applied. Our research, however, uncovered a few occasions when it worked masterfully. Take the case of a division president who was brought in to change the direction of a food company that was losing money. His first act was to have the executive conference room demolished. To him, the room—with its long marble table that looked like "the deck of the Starship Enterprise"—symbolized the tradition-bound formality that was paralyzing the company. The destruction of the room, and the subsequent move to a smaller, more informal setting, sent a message no one could miss, and the division's culture changed quickly in its wake.

That said, the coercive style should be used only with extreme caution and in the few situations when it is absolutely imperative, such as during a turnaround or when a hostile takeover is looming. In those cases, the coercive style can break failed business habits and shock people into new ways of working. It is always appropriate during a genuine emergency, like in the aftermath of an earthquake or a fire. And it can work with problem employees with whom all else has failed. But if a leader relies solely on this style or continues to use it once the emergency passes, the long-term impact of his insensitivity to the morale and feelings of those he leads will be ruinous.

THE AUTHORITATIVE STYLE

Tom was the vice president of marketing at a floundering national restaurant chain that specialized in pizza. Needless to say, the company's poor performance troubled the senior managers, but they were at a loss for what to do. Every Monday, they met to review recent sales, struggling to come up with fixes. To Tom, the approach didn't make sense. "We were always trying to figure out why our sales were down last week. We had the whole company looking backward instead of figuring out what we had to do tomorrow."

Tom saw an opportunity to change people's way of thinking at an off-site strategy meeting. There, the conversation began with stale truisms: the company had to drive up shareholder wealth and increase return on assets. Tom believed those concepts didn't have the power to inspire a restaurant manager to be innovative or to do better than a good-enough job.

So Tom made a bold move. In the middle of a meeting, he made an impassioned plea for his colleagues to think from the customer's perspective. Customers want convenience, he said. The company was not in the restaurant business, it was in the business of distributing high-quality, convenient-to-get pizza. That notion—and nothing else—should drive everything the company did.

With his vibrant enthusiasm and clear vision—the hallmarks of the authoritative style—Tom filled a leadership vacuum at the company. Indeed, his concept became the core of the new mission statement. But this conceptual breakthrough was just the beginning. Tom made sure that the mission statement was built into the company's strategic planning process as the designated driver of growth. And he ensured that the vision was articulated so that local restaurant managers understood they were the key to the company's success and were free to find new ways to distribute pizza.

Changes came quickly. Within weeks, many local managers started guaranteeing fast, new delivery times. Even better, they started to act like entrepreneurs, finding ingenious locations to open new branches: kiosks on busy street corners and in bus and train stations, even from carts in airports and hotel lobbies.

Tom's success was no fluke. Our research indicates that of the six leadership styles, the authoritative one is most effective, driving up every aspect of climate. Take clarity. The authoritative leader is a visionary; he motivates people by making clear to them how their work fits into a larger vision for the organization. People who work for such leaders understand that what they do matters and why. Authoritative

An authoritative leader states the end but gives people plenty of leeway to devise their own means.

leadership also maximizes commitment to the organization's goals and strategy. By framing the individual tasks within a grand vision, the authoritative leader defines standards that revolve around that vision. When he gives performance feedback—whether positive or negative—the singular criterion is whether or not that performance furthers the vision. The standards for success are clear to all, as are the rewards. Finally, consider the style's impact on flexibility. An authoritative leader states the end but generally gives people plenty of leeway to devise their own means. Authoritative leaders give people the freedom to innovate, experiment, and take calculated risks.

Because of its positive impact, the authoritative style works well in almost any business situation. But it is particularly effective when a business is adrift. An authoritative leader charts a new course and sells his people on a fresh long-term vision.

The authoritative style, powerful though it may be, will not work in every situation. The approach fails, for instance, when a leader is working with a team of experts or peers who are more experienced than he is; they may see the leader as pompous or out-of-touch. Another limitation: if a manager trying to be authoritative becomes overbearing, he can undermine the egalitarian spirit of an effective team. Yet even with such caveats, leaders would be wise to grab for the authoritative "club" more often than not. It may not guarantee a hole in one, but it certainly helps with the long drive.

THE AFFILIATIVE STYLE

If the coercive leader demands, "Do what I say," and the authoritative urges, "Come with me," the affiliative leader says, "People come first." This leadership style revolves around people—its proponents value individuals and their emotions more than tasks and goals. The affiliative leader strives to keep employees happy and to create harmony among them. He manages by building strong emotional bonds and then reaping the benefits of such an approach, namely fierce loyalty. The style also has a markedly positive effect on communication. People who like one another a lot talk a lot. They share ideas; they share inspiration. And the style drives up flexibility; friends trust one another, allowing habitual innovation and risk taking. Flexibility also rises because the affiliative leader, like a parent who adjusts household rules for a maturing adolescent, doesn't impose unnecessary strictures on how employees get their work done. They give people the freedom to do their job in the way they think is most effective.

As for a sense of recognition and reward for work well done, the affiliative leader offers ample positive feedback. Such feedback has special potency in the workplace because it is all too rare: outside of an annual review, most people usually get no feedback on their day-to-day efforts—or only negative feedback. That makes the affiliative leader's positive words all the more motivating. Finally, affiliative leaders are masters at building a sense of belonging. They are, for instance, likely to take their direct reports out for a meal or a drink, one-on-one, to see how they're doing. They will bring in a cake to celebrate a group accomplishment. They are natural relationship builders.

Joe Torre, the heart and soul of the New York Yankees, is a classic affiliative leader. During the 1999 World Series, Torre tended ably to the psyches of his players as they endured the emotional pressure cooker of a pennant race. All season long, he made a special point to praise Scott Brosius, whose father had died during the season, for staying committed even as he mourned. At the celebration party after the team's final game, Torre specifically sought out right fielder Paul O'Neill. Although he had received the news of his father's death that morning, O'Neill chose to play in the decisive game—and he burst into tears the moment it ended. Torre made a point of acknowledging O'Neill's personal struggle, calling him a "warrior." Torre also used the spotlight of the victory celebration to praise two players whose return the following year was threatened by contract disputes. In doing so, he sent a clear message to the team and to the club's owner that he valued the players immensely—too much to lose them.

Along with ministering to the emotions of his people, an affiliative leader may also tend to his own emotions openly. The year Torre's brother was near death awaiting a heart transplant, he shared his worries with his players. He also spoke candidly with the team about his treatment for prostate cancer.

The affiliative style's generally positive impact makes it a good all-weather approach, but leaders should employ it particularly when trying to build team harmony, increase morale, improve communication, or repair broken trust. For instance, one executive in our study was hired to replace a ruthless team leader. The former leader had taken credit for his employees' work and had attempted to pit them against one another. His efforts ultimately failed, but the team he left behind was suspicious and weary. The new executive managed to mend the situation by unstintingly showing emotional honesty and rebuilding ties. Several months in, her leadership had created a renewed sense of commitment and energy.

Despite its benefits, the affiliative style should not be used alone. Its exclusive focus on praise can allow poor performance to go uncorrected; employees may perceive that mediocrity is tolerated. And because affiliative leaders rarely offer constructive advice on how to improve, employees must figure out how to do so on their own. When people need clear directives to navigate through complex challenges, the affiliative style leaves them rudderless. Indeed, if overly relied on, this style can actually steer a group to failure. Perhaps that is why many affiliative leaders, including Torre, use this style in close conjunction with the authoritative style. Authoritative leaders state a vision, set standards, and let people know how their work is furthering the group's goals. Alternate that with the caring, nurturing approach of the affiliative leader, and you have a potent combination.

THE DEMOCRATIC STYLE

Sister Mary ran a Catholic school system in a large metropolitan area. One of the schools—the only private school in an impoverished neighborhood—had been losing money for years, and the archdiocese could no longer afford to keep it open. When Sister Mary eventually got the order to shut it down, she didn't just lock the doors. She called a meeting of all the teachers and staff at the school and explained to them the details of the financial crisis—the first time anyone working at the school had been included in the business side of the institution. She asked for their ideas on ways to keep the school open and on how to handle the closing, should it come to that. Sister Mary spent much of her time at the meeting just listening.

She did the same at later meetings for school parents and for the community and during a successive series of meetings for the school's teachers and staff. After two months of meetings, the consensus was clear: the school would have to close. A plan was made to transfer students to other schools in the Catholic system.

The final outcome was no different than if Sister Mary had gone ahead and closed the school the day she was told to. But by allowing the school's constituents to reach that decision collectively, Sister Mary received none of the backlash that would have accompanied such a move. People mourned the loss of the school, but they understood its inevitability. Virtually no one objected.

Compare that with the experiences of a priest in our research who headed another Catholic school. He, too, was told to shut it down. And he did—by fiat. The result was disastrous: parents filed lawsuits, teachers and parents picketed, and local newspapers ran editorials attacking his decision. It took a year to resolve the disputes before he could finally go ahead and close the school.

Sister Mary exemplifies the democratic style in action—and its benefits. By spending time getting people's ideas and buy-in, a leader builds trust, respect, and commitment. By letting workers themselves have a say in decisions that affect their goals and how they do their work, the democratic leader drives up flexibility and responsibility. And by listening to employees' concerns, the democratic leader learns what to do to keep morale high. Finally, because they have a say in setting their goals and the standards for evaluating success, people operating in a democratic system tend to be very realistic about what can and cannot be accomplished.

However, the democratic style has its drawbacks, which is why its impact on climate is not as high as some of the other styles. One of its more exasperating consequences can be endless meetings where ideas are mulled over, consensus remains elusive, and the only visible result is scheduling more meetings. Some democratic leaders use the style to put off making crucial decisions, hoping that enough thrashing things out will eventually yield a blinding insight. In reality, their people end up feeling confused and leaderless. Such an approach can even escalate conflicts.

When does the style work best? This approach is ideal when a leader is himself uncertain about the best direction to take and needs ideas and guidance from able employees. And even if a leader has a strong vision, the democratic style works well to generate fresh ideas for executing that vision.

The democratic style, of course, makes much less sense when employees are not competent or informed enough to offer sound advice. And it almost goes without saying that building consensus is wrongheaded in times of crisis. Take the case of a CEO whose computer company was severely threatened by changes in the market. He always sought consensus about what to do. As competitors stole customers and customers' needs changed, he kept appointing committees to consider the situation. When the market made a sudden shift because of a new technology, the CEO froze in his tracks. The board replaced him before he could appoint yet another task force to consider the situation. The new CEO, while occasionally democratic and affiliative, relied heavily on the authoritative style, especially in his first months.

THE PACESETTING STYLE

Like the coercive style, the pacesetting style has its place in the leader's repertory, but it should be used sparingly. That's not what we expected to find. After all, the hallmarks of the pacesetting style sound admirable. The leader sets extremely high performance standards and exemplifies them himself. He is obsessive about doing things better and faster, and he asks the same of everyone around him. He quickly pinpoints poor performers and demands more from them. If they don't rise to the occasion, he replaces them with people who can. You would think such an approach would improve results, but it doesn't.

In fact, the pacesetting style destroys climate. Many employees feel overwhelmed by the pacesetter's demands for excellence, and their morale drops. Guidelines for working may be clear in the leader's head, but she does not state them clearly; she expects people to know what to do and even thinks, "If I have to tell you, you're the wrong person for the job." Work becomes not a matter of doing one's best along a clear course so much as second-guessing what the leader wants. At the same time, people often feel that the pacesetter doesn't trust them to work in their own way or to take initiative. Flexibility and responsibility evaporate; work becomes so task focused and routinized it's boring.

As for rewards, the pacesetter either gives no feedback on how people are doing or jumps in to take over when he thinks they're lagging. And if the leader should leave, people feel directionless—they're so used to "the expert" setting the rules. Finally, commitment dwindles under the regime of a pacesetting leader because people have no sense of how their personal efforts fit into the big picture.

For an example of the pacesetting style, take the case of Sam, a biochemist in R&D at a large pharmaceutical company. Sam's superb technical expertise made him an early star: he was the one everyone turned to when they needed help. Soon he was promoted to head of a team developing a new product. The other scientists on the team were as competent and self-motivated as Sam; his métier as team leader became offering himself as a model of how to do first-class scientific work under tremendous deadline pressure, pitching in when needed. His team completed its task in record time.

But then came a new assignment: Sam was put in charge of R&D for his entire division. As his tasks expanded and he had to articulate a vision, coordinate projects, delegate responsibility, and help develop others, Sam began to slip. Not trusting that his subordinates were as capable as he was, he became a micromanager, obsessed with details and taking over for others when their performance slackened. Instead of trusting them to improve with guidance and development, Sam found himself working nights and weekends after stepping in to take over for the head of a floundering research team. Finally, his own boss suggested, to his relief, that he return to his old job as head of a product development team.

Although Sam faltered, the pacesetting style isn't always a disaster. The approach works well when all employees are self-motivated, highly competent, and need little direction or coordination—for example, it can work for leaders of highly skilled and self-motivated professionals, like R&D groups or legal teams. And, given a talented team to lead, pacesetting does exactly that: gets work done on time or even ahead of schedule. Yet like any leadership style, pacesetting should never be used by itself.

THE COACHING STYLE

A product unit at a global computer company had seen sales plummet from twice as much as its competitors to only half as much. So Lawrence, the president of the manufacturing division, decided to close the unit and reassign its people and products. Upon hearing the news, James, the head of the doomed unit, decided to go over his boss's head and plead his case to the CEO.

What did Lawrence do? Instead of blowing up at James, he sat down with his rebellious direct report and talked over not just the decision to close the division but also James's future. He explained to James how moving to another division would help him develop new skills. It would make him a better leader and teach him more about the company's business.

Lawrence acted more like a counselor than a traditional boss. He listened to James's concerns and hopes, and he shared his own. He said he believed James had grown stale in his current job; it was, after all, the only place he'd worked in the company. He predicted that James would blossom in a new role.

The conversation then took a practical turn. James had not yet had his meeting with the CEO—the one he had impetuously demanded when he heard of his division's closing. Knowing this—and also knowing that the CEO unwaveringly supported the closing—Lawrence took the time to coach James on how to present his case in that meeting. "You don't get an audience with the CEO very often," he noted, "let's make sure you impress him with your thoughtfulness." He advised James not to plead his personal case but to focus on the business unit: "If he thinks you're in there for your own glory, he'll throw you out faster than you walked through the door." And he urged him to put his ideas in writing; the CEO always appreciated that.

Lawrence's reason for coaching instead of scolding? "James is a good guy, very talented and promising," the executive explained to us, "and I don't want this to derail his career. I want him to stay with the company, I want him to work out, I want him to learn, I want him to benefit and grow. Just because he screwed up doesn't mean he's terrible."

Lawrence's actions illustrate the coaching style par excellence. Coaching leaders help employees identify their unique strengths and weaknesses and tie them to their personal and career aspirations. They encourage employees to establish long-term development goals and help them conceptualize a plan for attaining them. They make agreements with their employees about their role and responsibilities in enacting development plans, and they give plentiful instruction and feedback. Coaching leaders excel at delegating; they give employees challenging assignments, even if that means the tasks won't be accomplished quickly. In other words, these leaders are willing to put up with short-term failure if it furthers long-term learning.

Of the six styles, our research found that the coaching style is used least often. Many leaders told us they don't have the time in this high-pressure economy for the slow and tedious work of teaching people and helping them grow. But after a first session, it takes little or no extra time. Leaders who ignore this style are passing up a powerful tool: its impact on climate and performance are markedly positive.

Admittedly, there is a paradox in coaching's positive effect on business performance because coaching focuses primarily on personal development, not on immediate work-related tasks. Even so, coaching improves results. The reason: it requires constant dialogue, and that dialogue has a way of pushing up every driver of climate. Take flexibility. When an employee knows his boss watches him and cares about what he does, he feels free to experiment. After all, he's sure to get quick and constructive feedback. Similarly, the ongoing dialogue of coaching guarantees that people know what is expected of them and how their work fits into a larger vision or strategy. That affects responsibility and clarity. As for commitment, coaching helps there, too, because the style's implicit message is, "I believe in you, I'm investing in you, and I expect your best efforts." Employees very often rise to that challenge with their heart, mind, and soul.

The coaching style works well in many business situations, but it is perhaps most effective when people on the receiving end are "up for it." For instance, the coaching style works particularly well when employees are already aware of their weaknesses and would like to improve their performance. Similarly, the style works well when employees realize how cultivating new abilities can help them advance. In short, it works best with employees who want to be coached.

Leaders who have mastered four or more—especially the authoritative, democratic, affiliative, and coaching styles—have the best climate and business performance.

By contrast, the coaching style makes little sense when employees, for whatever reason, are resistant to learning or changing their ways. And it flops if the leader lacks the expertise to help the employee along. The fact is, many managers are unfamiliar with or simply inept at coaching, particularly when it comes to giving ongoing performance feedback that motivates rather than creates fear or apathy. Some companies have realized the positive impact of the style and are trying to make it a core competence. At some companies, a significant portion of annual bonuses are tied to an executive's development of his or her direct reports. But many organizations have yet to take full advantage of this leadership style. Although the coaching style may not scream "bottom-line results," it delivers them.

Leaders Need Many Styles

Many studies, including this one, have shown that the more styles a leader exhibits, the better. Leaders who have mastered four or more—especially the authoritative, democratic, affiliative, and coaching styles—have the very best climate and business performance. And the most effective leaders switch flexibly among the leadership styles as needed. Although that may sound daunting, we witnessed it more often than you might guess, at both large corporations and tiny start-ups, by seasoned veterans who could explain exactly how and why they lead and by entrepreneurs who claim to lead by gut alone.

Such leaders don't mechanically match their style to fit a checklist of situations—they are far more fluid. They are exquisitely sensitive to the impact they are having on others and seamlessly adjust their style to get the best results. These are leaders, for example, who can read in the first minutes of conversation that a talented but underperforming employee has been demoralized by an unsympathetic, do-it-the-way-I-tell-you manager and needs to be inspired through a reminder of why her work matters. Or that leader might choose to reenergize the employee by asking her about her dreams and aspirations and finding ways to make her job more challenging. Or that initial conversation might signal that the employee needs an ultimatum: improve or leave.

For an example of fluid leadership in action, consider Joan, the general manager of a major division at a global food and beverage company. Joan was appointed to her job while the division was in a deep crisis. It had not made its profit targets for six years; in the most recent year, it had missed by $50 million. Morale among the top management team was miserable; mistrust and resentments were rampant. Joan's directive from above was clear: turn the division around.

Joan did so with a nimbleness in switching among leadership styles that is rare. From the start, she realized she had a short window to demonstrate effective leadership and to establish rapport and trust. She also knew that she urgently needed to be informed about what was not working, so her first task was to listen to key people.

Her first week on the job she had lunch and dinner meetings with each member of the management team. Joan sought to get each person's understanding of the current situation. But her focus was not so much on learning how each person diagnosed the problem as on getting to know each manager as a person. Here Joan employed the affiliative style: she explored their lives, dreams, and aspirations.

She also stepped into the coaching role, looking for ways she could help the team members achieve what they wanted in their careers. For instance, one manager who had been getting feedback that he was a poor team player confided his worries to her. He thought he was a good team member, but he was plagued by persistent complaints. Recognizing that he was a talented executive and a valuable asset to the company, Joan made an agreement with him to point out (in private) when his actions undermined his goal of being seen as a team player.

She followed the one-on-one conversations with a three-day off-site meeting. Her goal here was team building, so that everyone would own whatever solution for the business problems emerged. Her initial stance at the off-site meeting was that of a democratic leader. She encouraged everyone to express freely their frustrations and complaints.

The next day, Joan had the group focus on solutions: each person made three specific proposals about what needed to be done. As Joan clustered the suggestions, a natural consensus emerged about priorities for the business, such as cutting costs. As the group came up with specific action plans, Joan got the commitment and buy-in she sought.

With that vision in place, Joan shifted into the authoritative style, assigning accountability for each follow-up step to specific executives and holding them responsible for their accomplishment. For example, the division had been dropping prices on products without increasing its volume. One obvious solution was to raise prices, but the previous VP of sales had dithered and had let the problem fester. The new VP of sales now had responsibility to adjust the price points to fix the problem.

Over the following months, Joan's main stance was authoritative. She continually articulated the group's new vision in a way that reminded each member of how his or her role was crucial to achieving these goals. And, especially during the first few weeks of the plan's implementation, Joan felt that the urgency of the business crisis justified an occasional shift into the coercive style should someone fail to meet his or her responsibility. As she put it, "I had to be brutal about this follow-up and make sure this stuff happened. It was going to take discipline and focus."

The results? Every aspect of climate improved. People were innovating. They were talking about the division's vision and crowing about their commitment to new, clear goals. The ultimate proof of Joan's fluid leadership style is written in black ink: after only seven months, her division exceeded its yearly profit target by $5 million.

Expanding Your Repertory

Few leaders, of course, have all six styles in their repertory, and even fewer know when and how to use them. In fact, as we have brought the findings of our research into many organizations, the most common responses have been, "But I have only two of those!" and, "I can't use all those styles. It wouldn't be natural."

Such feelings are understandable, and in some cases, the antidote is relatively simple. The leader can build a team with members who employ styles she lacks. Take the case of a VP for manufacturing. She successfully ran a global factory system largely by using the affiliative style. She was on the road constantly, meeting with plant managers, attending to their pressing concerns, and letting them know how much she cared about them personally. She left the division's strategy—extreme efficiency—to a trusted lieutenant with a keen understanding of technology, and she delegated its performance standards to a colleague who was adept at the authoritative approach. She also had a pacesetter on her team who always visited the plants with her.

An alternative approach, and one I would recommend more, is for leaders to expand their own style repertories. To do so, leaders must first understand which emotional intelligence competencies underlie the leadership styles they are lacking. They can then work assiduously to increase their quotient of them.

For instance, an affiliative leader has strengths in three emotional intelligence competencies: in empathy, in building relationships, and in communication. Empathy—sensing how people are feeling in the moment— allows the affiliative leader to respond to employees in a way that is highly congruent with that person's emotions, thus building rapport. The affiliative leader also displays a natural ease in forming new relationships, getting to know someone as a person, and cultivating a bond. Finally, the outstanding affiliative leader has mastered the art of interpersonal communication, particularly in saying just the right thing or making the apt symbolic gesture at just the right moment.

So if you are primarily a pacesetting leader who wants to be able to use the affiliative style more often, you would need to improve your level of empathy and, perhaps, your skills at building relationships or communicating effectively. As another example, an authoritative leader who wants to add the democratic style to his repertory might need to work on the capabilities of collaboration and communication. Such advice about adding capabilities may seem simplistic—"Go change yourself"—but enhancing emotional intelligence is entirely possible with practice. (For more on how to improve emotional intelligence, see "Growing Your Emotional Intelligence" at the end of this article.)

More Science, Less Art

Like parenthood, leadership will never be an exact science. But neither should it be a complete mystery to those who practice it. In recent years, research has helped parents understand the genetic, psychological, and behavioral components that affect their "job performance." With our new research, leaders, too, can get a clearer picture of what it takes to lead effectively. And perhaps as important, they can see how they can make that happen.

The business environment is continually changing, and a leader must respond in kind. Hour to hour, day to day, week to week, executives must play their leadership styles like a pro—using the right one at just the right time and in the right measure. The payoff is in the results.

Notes

1. Daniel Goleman consults with Hay/McBer on leadership development.

Emotional Intelligence: A Primer

EMOTIONAL INTELLIGENCE—the ability to manage ourselves and our relationships effectively—consists of four fundamental capabilities: self-awareness, self-management, social awareness, and social skill. Each capability, in turn, is composed of specific sets of competencies. Below is a list of the capabilities and their corresponding traits.

Self-Awareness

- *Emotional self-awareness:* the ability to read and understand your emotions as well as recognize their impact on work performance, relationships, and the like.

- *Accurate self-assessment:* a realistic evaluation of your strengths and limitations.

- *Self-confidence:* a strong and positive sense of self-worth.

Self-Management

- *Self-control:* the ability to keep disruptive emotions and impulses under control.
- *Trustworthiness:* a consistent display of honesty and integrity.
- *Conscientiousness:* the ability to manage yourself and your responsibilities.
- *Adaptability:* skill at adjusting to changing situations and overcoming obstacles.
- *Achievement orientation:* the drive to meet an internal standard of excellence.
- *Initiative:* a readiness to seize opportunities.

Social Awareness

- *Empathy:* skill at sensing other people's emotions, understanding their perspective, and taking an active interest in their concerns.
- *Organizational awareness:* the ability to read the currents of organizational life, build decision networks, and navigate politics.
- *Service orientation:* the ability to recognize and meet customers' needs.

Social Skill

- *Visionary leadership:* the ability to take charge and inspire with a compelling vision.
- *Influence:* the ability to wield a range of persuasive tactics.
- *Developing others:* the propensity to bolster the abilities of others through feedback and guidance.

- **Communication:** skill at listening and at sending clear, convincing, and well-tuned messages.

- **Change catalyst:** proficiency in initiating new ideas and leading people in a new direction.

- **Conflict management:** the ability to de-escalate disagreements and orchestrate resolutions.

- **Building bonds:** proficiency at cultivating and maintaining a web of relationships.

- **Teamwork and collaboration:** competence at promoting cooperation and building teams.

Growing Your Emotional Intelligence

UNLIKE IQ, which is largely genetic—it changes little from childhood—the skills of emotional intelligence can be learned at any age. It's not easy, however. Growing your emotional intelligence takes practice and commitment. But the payoffs are well worth the investment.

Consider the case of a marketing director for a division of a global food company. Jack, as I'll call him, was a classic pacesetter: high-energy, always striving to find better ways to get things done, and too eager to step in and take over when, say, someone seemed about to miss a deadline. Worse, Jack was prone to pounce on anyone who didn't seem to meet his standards, flying off the handle if a person merely deviated from completing a job in the order Jack thought best.

Jack's leadership style had a predictably disastrous impact on climate and business results. After two years of stagnant performance, Jack's boss suggested he seek out a coach. Jack wasn't pleased but, realizing his own job was on the line, he complied.

The coach, an expert in teaching people how to increase their emotional intelligence, began with a 360-degree evaluation of Jack. A diagnosis from multiple viewpoints is essential in improving emotional intelligence because those who need the most help usually have blind spots. In fact, our research found that top-performing leaders overestimate their strengths on, at most, one emotional intelligence ability, whereas poor performers overrate themselves on four or more. Jack was not that far off, but he did rate himself more glowingly than his direct reports, who gave him especially low grades on emotional self-control and empathy.

Initially, Jack had some trouble accepting the feedback data. But when his coach showed him how those weaknesses were tied to his inability to display leadership styles dependent on those competencies—especially the authoritative, affiliative, and coaching styles—Jack realized he had to improve if he wanted to advance in the company. Making such a connection is essential. The reason: improving emotional intelligence isn't done in a weekend or during a seminar—it takes diligent practice on the job, over several months. If people do not see the value of the change, they will not make that effort.

Once Jack zeroed in on areas for improvement and committed himself to making the effort, he and his coach worked up a plan to turn his day-to-day job into a learning laboratory. For instance, Jack discovered he was empathetic when things were calm, but in a crisis, he tuned out others. This tendency hampered his ability to listen to what people were telling him in the very moments he most needed to do so. Jack's plan required him to focus on his behavior during tough situations. As soon as he felt himself tensing up, his job was to immediately step back, let the other person speak, and then ask clarifying questions. The point was to not act judgmental or hostile under pressure.

The change didn't come easily, but with practice Jack learned to defuse his flare-ups by entering into a dialogue instead of launching a harangue. Although he didn't always agree with them, at least he gave people a chance to make their case. At the same time, Jack also practiced giving his direct reports more positive feedback and reminding them of how their work contributed to the group's mission. And he restrained himself from micromanaging them.

Jack met with his coach every week or two to review his progress and get advice on specific problems. For instance, occasionally Jack would find himself falling back on his old pacesetting tactics—cutting people off, jumping in to take over, and blowing up in a rage. Almost immediately, he would regret it. So he and his coach dissected those relapses to figure out what triggered the old ways and what to do the next time a similar moment arose. Such "relapse prevention" measures inoculate people against future lapses or just giving up. Over a six-month period, Jack made real improvement. His own records showed he had reduced the number of flare-ups from one or more a day at the beginning to just one or two a month. The climate had improved sharply, and the division's numbers were starting to creep upward.

Why does improving an emotional intelligence competence take months rather than days? Because the emotional centers of the brain, not just the neocortex, are involved. The neocortex, the thinking brain that learns technical skills and purely cognitive abilities, gains knowledge very quickly, but the emotional brain does not. To master a new behavior, the emotional centers need repetition and practice. Improving your emotional intelligence, then, is akin to changing your habits. Brain circuits that carry leadership habits have to unlearn the old ones and replace them with the new. The more often a behavioral sequence is repeated, the stronger the underlying brain circuits become. At some point, the new neural pathways become the brain's default option. When that happened, Jack was able to go through the paces of leadership effortlessly, using styles that worked for him— and the whole company.

Originally published in March–April 2000
Reprint R00204

Getting the Attention You Need

THOMAS H. DAVENPORT AND JOHN C. BECK

Executive Summary

EMPLOYEES HAVE AN ENORMOUS amount of business information at their fingertips—more specifically, at their desktops. The floodgates are open; profitable possibilities abound. But having to handle all that information has pushed downsized staffs to the brink of an acute attention deficit disorder. To achieve corporate goals, business leaders need their employees' full attention—and that attention is in short supply.

Authors Thomas Davenport and John Beck have studied how companies manage the attention of their employees and their site visitors. In this article, they analyze the components of attention management through three lenses—economic, psychobiological, and technological—and offer guidelines for keeping employees focused on crucial corporate tasks. Their lessons are drawn from the best practices employed by today's stickiest Web sites and by traditional attention industries such as advertising, film, and television.

The authors say executives must manage attention knowing that it's a zero-sum game (there's only so much to go around). Managers should also consider capitalizing on the basic survival and competitive instincts we all have that help determine how much attention we pay to certain things. For instance, the threat of corporate demise—and the consequent loss of jobs and livelihoods—undoubtedly focuses worker's attention on the need to change. Likewise, internal competition among business units may give employees added incentive to pay attention to a profit or sales goal.

Leaders today need to pay more attention to attention because it's widely misunderstood and widely mismanaged, the authors conclude.

BUSINESS LEADERS CAN'T ACCOMPLISH anything if their employees aren't paying attention; to achieve long-term and short-term corporate goals, leaders need their people to focus in a sustained way on those goals.

Leaders today need to pay more attention to attention because it is widely misunderstood and widely mismanaged.

And lately, a lot of people's attention is wandering. It's easy to see why. Bill Gates's dream that we'd have all the information we want at our fingertips has come true with a vengeance. Intranets, software applications, and portals continually wash tsunamis of information onto our desktops. The average manager receives more than 100 voice mail and e-mail messages a day. It would be bad enough if all this information were flung at a steady state audience, but in many organizations, staffs are leaner than ever. More information, fewer people—it's no wonder that so many companies are on the verge of an acute attention deficit disorder.

Over the past several years, we've studied attention management, looking at how well—and how poorly—it is practiced in traditional organizations and on the World Wide Web. We've analyzed attention management using three lenses: the economic, the psychobiological, and the technological. One overarching lesson has emerged from our research: leaders today need to pay more attention to attention because it is widely misunderstood and widely mismanaged. People may be paying attention to all the information coming at them but rarely in the ways that leaders would want or expect.

In this article, we'll explore the economic, psychobiological, and technological perspectives on attention management, and we'll identify the operating principles they suggest. Interestingly, while attention management has been around for thousands of years—think Moses on Mount Sinai or Winston Churchill in the darkest hours of World War II—some of the most powerful tactics we've observed come from the new adventurers on the Web. Not all, however. Lessons from the advertising, television, and film industries can also help executives as they try to manage one of their scarcest resources: the full engagement of employees' minds. (See "Lessons from the Attention Industries" at the end of this article.)

The Economics of Attention

Is it hyperbolic to suggest that we're living in an attention economy? Not in our opinion. Economics, by definition, is the study of how whole societies allocate scarce resources. The scarcest resource for today's business leaders is no longer just land, capital, or human labor, and it certainly isn't information. Attention is what's in short supply. And human attention certainly behaves like an economic good in the sense that we buy it and measure it. On an individual level, we're deeply aware when we don't have enough of it—which suggests the first lesson of attention management.

Manage attention knowing that it's a zero-sum game; there's only so much to go around. People may not think of their own attention as a scarce economic good, but they certainly act as though it is. They don't want their time, or their attention, wasted.

The best Web sites have capitalized on this principle. The stickiest sites—meaning the URLs that visitors tend to click on, stay at for a while, and return to time and time again—provide high returns on attention investment, usually measured in time savings for the user. For instance, Yahoo! is a hugely successful search engine because its human-based approach to classifying sites yields fewer irrelevant "hits" than a computer-based approach and promises a less complex search. More generally, our research suggests that Web users value portals not because they want access to many sites but because the portals provide efficient access to the few sites that interest them. And when Web sites sell products or services, users tend to reward easy transactions, straightforward navigation, and access to a variety of goods. Again, the attraction for users is a high return on attention investment, and managers at sticky sites like Amazon.com and eBay actively strategize toward this goal.

The most important implication of the zero-sum rule for managers at traditional organizations is that they need to limit the number of internal programs that compete for employees' attention. We can't overstate the importance of this point. One Harvard professor's informal survey suggested that the average company has more than 16 major initiatives under way at any given time—for instance, implementing new technologies or restructuring a functional unit. Many businesspeople we speak with complain of "initiative fatigue" and say they just can't pay attention to all of them. Wise leaders understand the danger of spreading attention too thin. When they introduce a new initiative, they retire an old one. It's as simple as that. For example, when BP acquired Amoco and then Atlantic Richfield, senior executives were concerned that managers would be distracted by too much information, at a time when oil prices were very low. So BP halved the number of its IT applications to cut down on the information those applications produced.

But what happens if several strategic imperatives cry out for attention at once? This happened recently at Clarica, formerly Mutual Life of Canada, a large Canadian insurance company that went through two major changes, one in 1998 and one in 1999. The company had announced its intention to demutualize—in other words, to change its ownership by policyholders to ownership by public stock. This is a complex and difficult transition, involving regulatory, financial, and customer relationship changes. Insurance companies prepare for it for months and years, and it monopolizes senior management's attention.

A few months into the demutualization process, another major opportunity emerged. Metropolitan Life, the largest U.S. insurer, decided to sell its Canadian business and announced that it was taking bids. The possibility of buying the MetLife business, which would increase by half Clarica's customers and assets, presented an "attention crisis" for CEO Bob Astley and the executive team. They didn't feel they had enough senior management attention left to undertake the deal's due diligence process, make the bid, and integrate the business with Clarica if their bid was successful.

One of the most important factors for gaining and sustaining attention is engaging people's emotions.

The demand for attention dictated the need for a new supply of it. Astley and his team decided to deputize 150 second-level managers to work on different aspects of the MetLife acquisition. Hubert St. Onge, senior vice president of strategic resources, led the effort. As a result, the senior team continued to focus most of its attention on the demutualization process. Every Saturday, they met for several hours to be briefed on the acquisition. After Clarica's bid was accepted, an Integration Management Office was formed to merge the two organizations; the office required little of senior management's attention. Eventually, both the demutualization process and the MetLife acquisition were completed, and the acquisition and integration of the new business were completed ahead of schedule. Those successes can be traced back, in large part, to senior management's intelligent allocation of its own attention.

The Psychobiology of Attention

Seeing attention purely through an economic lens distorts its reality somewhat. Economics, after all, assumes that rational actors make deliberate investment choices to optimize their returns. In reality, much of what determines where people invest their attention is below the level of pure reason. Indeed, our research suggests that one of the most important factors for gaining and sustaining attention is engaging people's emotions.

Allow us to predict one specific behavior, based on the psychobiology of attention: no matter what business activity you are involved in—sitting in a meeting, making a decision, or reading the *Wall Street Journal*—you would stop that activity immediately if a snake slithered into the room. Over millennia of focusing on life-and-death issues, our nervous systems have evolved to pay attention to some things more than others. Aspiring attention managers should be at least as attuned to the psychobiology of attention as they are to its economics. There are four linked lessons from psychobiology.

People are hardwired to fight for survival; use that to your benefit. All primates are biologically programmed not simply to fear snakes but to pay close attention to them. Web designers and business managers alike can use that natural reaction to get and hold onto people's attention.

On-line grocery shopping in Brazil illustrates the point. Brazilians became so accustomed to hyperinflation over the years that when they got a paycheck, they'd immediately buy vast quantities of groceries. Who knew how much the check would be worth in one day, let alone after a whole month? Even though inflation has been tamed, Brazilians still buy groceries in huge quantities. On-line retailers there have noted this survival reaction and have exploited it. By far, the largest e-commerce category in Brazil is grocery sales: they constitute 39% of total e-commerce in Brazil versus 3.4% in the U.S.

In organizations, the psychobiology of survival is obvious in the strategies managers use to get and keep workforce attention. The threat of corporate demise—and the consequent loss of jobs and livelihoods—focuses attention on the need to change. But that attention must be managed carefully, lest people become paralyzed by fear rather than attentive to it. Employees find new jobs, or they hunker down and get ready to change. Either way, you can be sure they are paying attention. When Japanese automakers threatened to drive Ford out of business in the early 1980s, senior managers and employees were motivated to pay attention to quality and efficiency in a way they never had before. Suddenly product and process design became high priorities. By the end of that decade, an MIT study rated Ford facilities as the highest-quality plants in the world.

In short, scaring your employees is a great way to get their attention. But make sure the threat is genuine, and don't use this tactic too often. If you do, your employees will stop believing that the threat is real.

People are naturally competitive; use that to your benefit, as well. Competitive urges are part instinct, part cultural conditioning, and eminently exploitable. Sports and investment Web sites play to those urges indirectly by providing the latest scores, stock prices, and predictions. And some of the stickiest Web sites involve outright competition. For instance, at Lycos's Gamesville.com, participants compete against thousands of other players who are simultaneously logged on to the Web site. Players return to the site again and again to have fun, to beat their neighbors at backgammon, and to win prizes. Even though the prizes are small—typically $1 to $5—Lycos's executives think they're one key to the site's success.

Competition can also focus people on a business goal. There's no question, for instance, that the Malcolm Baldrige Award has helped employees at quality-minded organizations keep their eyes on the prize. The concept can be taken too far if internal competition—to be the unit that creates most value, for instance—begins to produce divisiveness. But the chances are good that a bit of rivalry will make the work more compelling to everyone.

Smart leaders find ways to keep employees laser-focused on their business competitors, too. During a period of economic doldrums for Motorola during the mid-1990s, executives in one cellular-phone division were encouraged to carry a pager that periodically announced stock prices for Motorola, Ericsson, AT&T, and Nokia. Every time a competitor's stock price jumped significantly, pagers would beep or vibrate and everyone in the room would know they were in a tough battle— and that the stock market was giving Motorola's competitors a lot of credit. At the time, the pagers didn't go off much for Motorola stock increases. But partly because of employees' competitiveness, Motorola experienced rapid shareholder increases the next two years.

Don't let distractions keep people away from your core message. If you want to catch a raccoon, show him a shiny object to distract him. People, like raccoons, are infinitely distractible, and that's the biggest problem in this age of attention deficit.

On the Web, distractibility cuts both ways: banner advertising, for example, is the number one source of revenue, and it's also the number one distraction for users. One of the most popular banner ads of 1999 featured an animated monkey quickly bounding across the top of the screen. If you "punched the monkey" by clicking on it, you were whisked to a gambling site. Many people found the manic monkey an irresistible target. Great news for the gambling site—but mixed news for the sites running that ad.

In most organizations, the worst distraction is one we mentioned previously—the multiple internal programs that compete for employees' attention. But they're hardly the only distraction. For example, when the Chemical and Manufacturers Hanover banks agreed to merge several years ago, employees at both banks were justifiably concerned about their futures. Bruce Hasenyager, an IT executive at Chemical, noticed that productivity was slumping because employees were gossiping and exchanging rumors. He created "Rumor Mill," a discussion database that allowed any IT employee to describe a rumor that he or she had heard about the merger. Hasenyager promised that he would address any rumor about which he had information. While some executives were uncomfortable with the discussion, Hasenyager believed that deflating all the speculation made it easier for employees to get back to work.

Other companies attack distractions by offering to help employees with their personal chores. For example, concierge services are available to stand in line at the registry of motor vehicles or to pick up dry cleaning so that overextended employees can focus on their work.

People want to feel engaged, so help make that happen. If you can get people to invest something of their own, they're going to be more committed than if they feel like observers. That's the main force behind the stickiness of investment sites like Fidelity's and Schwab's, event-tracking sites like When.com, and any site that makes heavy use of on-line discussion. Co-creation pulls people in. It makes people feel like they count, and it makes it harder for them to disengage. Personalization and customization are forms of cocreation because they require the site user to invest some time to report their preferences for the type of service they'll receive. A perfect example is MyYahoo!.com, which allows a sports fan to position sports news at the top of his or her personalized home page, or a homesick expatriate to highlight all the news from Ohio—and requires both of them to share information and invest time with the Web site up front.

Amazon.com is often cited as another champion of cocreation, since it relies on reader-submitted reviews to provide other site visitors with rich content. The success of the tactic may actually have more to do with the flattery and recognition that the user doing the posting receives than on the content itself. Amazon also relies on personalization techniques to get users' attention, beginning with the cheery "Hello John Smith!" that greets John when he logs on. At a deeper level, the site targets returning customers by recommending books or other items based on past purchases.

Personalization requires relatively sophisticated technology and a labor-intensive approach to content, which is why more Web sites don't do it. Yet our research suggests that when people have too much information to process, personalization is one of the most important factors in their choice to attend to one piece of information over another. (See "What Kind of Message Gets Attention?" at the end of this article.)

Cocreation works inside businesses, too. Employees who have helped to make something happen stay invested, and they stay interested. One of the best examples we've discovered is Texas Instruments, whose CEO made it a top priority in 1994 for the company to define its new vision and strategic plan. To ensure that the plan got the attention it deserved, he put not only his strategic leadership team on the hook for it, but also a broader group of vice presidents, senior vice presidents, and other employees. And the process didn't end there. Once an initial draft was produced, more than 200 other TI executives were invited to participate in shaping it. Senior managers could have just herded this second tier of employees into a large room and asked for comments, but they didn't. Instead, they orchestrated a series of five-day events for groups of 25 to 30 managers and revealed the draft strategic vision only after two full days of exploring competitive dynamics and explaining the process that resulted in the vision proposal. At that point, participants had the knowledge base and the confidence to offer thoughtful criticisms and recommendations, which were readily incorporated into the final product.

One TI executive reported that this inclusive process had multiple benefits. It helped keep the strategic vision alive when the CEO died unexpectedly: "Two or three hundred of us had worked on this. We didn't want to just move forward with it—we wanted to pick up the pace." The process also helped TI gain consensus quickly on the divestiture of a financially successful business unit that didn't fit the strategy. Even the heads of the unit in question, who'd been among the original strategists, agreed with the divestiture.

Personalization can also be a powerful tool for getting and holding employees' attention. At one company, the CEO recently sent each employee a letter at home stating how much revenues needed to increase in the last quarter to meet a growth goal—and exactly how much bigger the individual's bonus would be if that goal was reached. Previously, only the top people would have received a letter of that kind; it used to be considered too expensive to personalize a mass mailing. Employees overwhelmingly agreed that the letters had focused them mightily on their tasks—and the goals were met.

Technologies and Attention

Technologies offer extraordinarily rich ways to capture people's attention. This has been true throughout human history: the Protestant Reformation wouldn't have happened without the distribution of Bibles, for example, and the French and American revolutions wouldn't have happened without newspapers. The invention of the printing press made both media possible.

Today, businesses use dozens of technologies and media to attract attention. Burson-Marsteller, a global communications firm, prepares both internal and external communications campaigns for its clients. PR has traditionally focused on broadcasting messages outside the company using a variety of media. But now multimedia technologies are being employed to communicate both internal and external messages.

Burson has one client, a financial services firm, whose managers concluded that if they wanted to get the attention of analysts, bankers, and traders, e-mail was not enough; communications had to be face to face. The company now uses a combination of worldwide satellite broadcasts and streaming video Webcasts, sometimes with simultaneous translation of the audio stream into multiple languages. The same broadcast may be viewed by investment analysts and employees.

Many companies now use worldwide videoconferences to distribute important messages to those who weren't closely involved in creating them. Sometimes the broadcasts are augmented with anonymous Web chat rooms, in which the participants can say what they really think about their leaders' messages—and such candid feedback tends to get the leaders' attention in return. In another example, Hewlett-Packard issues audiocassettes about new initiatives and programs for employees to listen to while they're commuting. Despite all these potential improvements to communication, we have two cautionary notes about technology and attention.

Don't let technology get in the way. Something that appears to be a great attention-getting technology can be worse than useless if it's supported by an insufficient infrastructure. Web users outside the United States often talk about whether the country is "awake yet" before logging on, because heavy Internet usage during U.S. daytime hours slows down so many sites. Multiple formats and complex technologies for playing sound and video over the Web may draw attention to a site, but they may destroy its capacity to sustain attention.

Similar problems crop up at traditional companies. Managers promoting a new venture or initiative often don't realize that, even as they are asking people to behave in a new way, they are making it difficult for that to happen. For instance, different e-mail systems and incompatible releases of crucial software programs make it nearly impossible for workers to get up to speed with a new initiative. One German multinational we worked with had launched a knowledge management project designed to let employees and customers share information seamlessly. This initiative was central to the company's larger goal—to change from a company that sold products into one that sold knowledge-based services. The problem was there were two competing versions of the software the company was using for knowledge management. One, in German, was based in Germany. The other, in English, was global. Neither flourished, partly because nobody could figure out which version of the software to use.

Don't get into a technology arms race. The standard for what gets attention is always being raised; what was dazzling yesterday is boring today. On the Web, for example, it used to be de rigueur to divide the page into browsable sections, or frames, even though the frames were confusing and slow to download. Today, frames are as outdated as hula hoops.

The same holds true for company communications. At one point, inserting into a presentation cute clip art of a duck bashing a computer with a sledgehammer could get your audience's rapt attention—and a few chuckles besides. Now, every person with a computer uses the same goofy clips in their presentations, along with the same artful backgrounds, the same fonts, the same snazzy transitions between slides. If you're talking about newsletters, everybody's got the same crisp, Page-Maker-supplied, multicolumn formats. Even video is becoming a commodity. Sun Microsystems CEO Scott McNealy realized that this kind of arms race was counterproductive and banned PowerPoint presentations at the company.

Sustaining Attention

Getting employees to stick to important strategic initiatives—and to give those initiatives their undivided attention over time—is crucial to competing successfully today.

In discussing the factors that contribute to sustained attention, we've focused on elements different from those required for capturing attention in the first place. We should point out that the tactics that lure a Web user to a site for the first time—or an employee to focus on a strategic initiative in the first place—are not the same as the ones that will keep them coming back. Stickiness as measured on the Web is usually a combination of the number of unique visits to the site and the total time spent by the average user across multiple visits, but the factors that create those behaviors are not the same.

The difference between capturing attention in the first place and sustaining it is nothing short of the difference between making a promise and keeping it.

In the organizational setting, managers have succeeded all too well in getting that first bite—and the result is that workers everywhere have become as immune to management's messages as the neighbors of the boy who cried wolf did. The difference between capturing attention in the first place and sustaining it is nothing short of the difference between making a promise and keeping it. It's far more important to do the latter. Management must set the right example if it wants a focused, committed workforce.

In the industrial economy, attention wasn't the scarce resource that it is today. There were more people to do the same amount of work, or even less work. Business wasn't as complex and didn't change as quickly, and knowledge workers weren't at the core of sophisticated economies. Information was scarce, and so we pursued hardware and software strategies that made vast amounts of information available at every desktop. With an enormous boost from the Internet, we were successful beyond our wildest dreams. Now it's human attention that's scarce, and our entire view of business needs to change. When we ask ourselves what's the constraining factor in the success of new business strategies, marketing campaigns, or knowledge management initiatives, the answer is likely to be attention. In the attention economy, we will have to evaluate every action with regard to how much attention it will consume and how we can get and keep the attention we need.

Lessons from the Attention Industries

SOME INDUSTRIES, such as advertising, television, film, and print have grown up learning to capture and sustain attention. Managers in other industries can benefit from what they've learned.

Advertising

Advertising, which is about very little else but attracting and sustaining attention, offers managers three important points to ponder. First, good advertisers measure everything. Devices that measure how many viewers are watching a TV program were developed primarily for the benefit of the advertising industry, for example. A good agency knows exactly which ads pull in which consumers, how much those consumers spend, and what their return rates are. We've only started to learn to measure employees' attention; getting better at it will pay off in a big way. (See "Measuring Attention.")

Second, agencies have long counseled that an advertising message should be delivered through multiple media—TV, newspapers and magazines, billboards, video screens at gas station pumps, and so on. Internet banner advertising is in that mix. If senior managers want to get an important message across to their people, they also need to employ multiple media. Executives at the software company Symantec, for example, received complaints from employees about poor internal communications—which were primarily by e-mail. They concluded that crucial messages should be sent through executive speeches, e-mail, paper memos, and express mailings of documents and videotapes to employees' homes.

And third, advertisers are virtually unanimous on the importance of a clear message, repeated often. If you're going to get consumers' attention and change their behavior, it's got to be obvious what you want them to do. Companies, too, must focus attention on a small set of clear ideas. CEO Jack Welch is extremely effective at focusing the attention of GE employees on a single critical topic. This year, it's "destroy your business.com," an initiative to understand how GE business units can compete using electronic commerce. Previously, Welch had targeted improved quality through the use of Six Sigma standards, increased inventory turns, and the elimination of unnecessary work. Like a good advertiser, he repeats the message in speeches, in one-on-one meetings with managers, in annual reports, and in press interviews. A GE employee who doesn't want to heed the message would have a tough time avoiding it.

Television

Television, which is still stickier than the Internet overall—the average American watches TV for three hours and 26 minutes per day—offers some lessons of its own. Take program scheduling: a network's promising new shows are typically slated to follow proven winners. Even the highly structured, predictable nature of TV programs over time is a factor in managing viewers' attention. Learning from that, executives in companies should schedule their communications at regular intervals—for instance, sending e-mails that summarize the previous week's performance every Monday at 9 A.M. Television programs also rely heavily on narrative and storytelling. Their success may account for the rise of storytelling in business. 3M, for example, has had great success adapting its strategic planning process to a storytelling format. (For more details, see Gordon Shaw, Robert Brown, and Philip Bromley's "Strategic Stories: How 3M is Rewriting Business Planning," HBR May–June 1998.)

Film

In darkened theaters around the world, we sit like zombies, our attention totally focused on projected images and recorded sounds. One of the most important lessons from the film industry is that people actually like the "captive attention" environment of the theater—as long as they are entertained. This bodes well for those who want to manage attention, though it also shows how high the entertainment value of a message must be to capture people's focus.

Movies also illustrate the importance of age segmentation in attention management. Attention allocation is different for people at different ages and from different environments. Web companies like iTurf and Yahoo! are just now beginning to focus on the attention market for teens and preteens, which movies have monopolized for years. Companies must be careful about segmenting their internal communications according to age because of discrimination issues, but the crafty communicator might avoid that problem by segmenting according to level or rank. If you're sending a message to lower-level employees who are likely to be young, make the communication as flashy and colorful as you can. For higher-level executives, you may still get away with black-and-white text.

Print

Magazines and books prosper when they embrace the "cult of personality," glorifying authors and the subjects they cover. In 1999, there were more new magazines about media personalities than in any other category, and the best-selling books were by celebrity authors such as Stephen King and John Grisham.

The literature on leadership is full of discussions about the virtues—and problems—of charismatic CEOs. Steve Jobs at Apple, Lee Iacocca at Chrysler, and Ross Perot at EDS and Perot Systems demonstrated the attention-getting potential of a "star" leader. Hewlett-Packard is attempting to make its latest CEO, Carly Fiorina, an executive celebrity by featuring her in TV ads. And managers inside the company say she's getting more internal attention than any CEO has since HP's founders because she's orchestrated this major communications campaign.

What Kind of Message Gets Attention?

WE SURVEYED 60 executives, asking each of them to track every message they received for one week and to rate how well each message attracted their attention. For the messages that received a high level of attention, we asked about the attributes of the message. Overall, the factors most highly associated with getting their attention, in rank order, were: the message was personalized, it evoked an emotional response, it came from a trustworthy or respected sender, and it was concise. The messages that both evoked emotion and were personalized were more than twice as likely to be attended to as the messages without those attributes.

Almost half the messages that got high levels of attention were e-mails, while only 16% were voice mail messages. Messages in other media grabbed even less attention. Several factors were not correlated with attention impact: whether the message came from a superior, whether the information was new or unusual, and whether the recipient agreed with the sender about the content of the message.

Measuring Attention

The same things that make for sticky Web sites make for sticky business in general because the same conditions of attention deficit prevail. So why has "stickiness" become such a Web-specific buzzword? One simple reason is that the attributes of the Internet make it uniquely capable of measuring stickiness.

We believe that attention in a business can be measured, albeit not with the precision that it's measured online. We've relied thus far on getting people to report on their own mental processes. We've developed the AttentionScape, one of several tools that we've used in our research, which maps the way a person allocates his or her attention. It's based on the fact that there are six types of attention that anyone can give to any issue or item; the six types represent the opposite extremes in three categories. Attention can be voluntary or captive; aversive or attractive; and front-of-mind or back-of-mind. Attention is maximized by appealing to all six types, which isn't as paradoxical as it sounds. A movie trailer may command your captive attention, because you're sitting in a dark room and have been shamed into silence, and your voluntary attention, because the preview turns out to be pretty engaging—both at the same time. Employees are most productive when they feel the right mix of stress (what we consider aversive attention) and reward (what we consider attractive attention). You want your employees' work to have highly engaging front-of-mind elements as well as routine back-of-mind elements. And there should be some parts of the job that they feel they cannot escape and some parts they're crazy about.

The AttentionScape was designed to reveal the type of attention an individual—or a team or a corporation—pays to a particular issue at a given time, using a chart like the one at right. The size of the bubbles indicates the amount of attention devoted to the issue. The X axis plots the amount of captive versus voluntary attention a user experiences. (If they are balanced equally, the attention bubble is at the center of the axis lines.) The Y axis plots front-of-mind versus back-of-mind attention. And the shade of the bubbles indicates attractive attention (darker shades) versus aversive attention (lighter shades).

The chart we show here measures responses from Sally B. Goode, an executive at a software company called FloppyTech. Sally answered several questions about her daily tasks and responsibilities, and she reported the time and attention she paid to each. For each task, there is a shaded bubble on Sally's Attention-Scape chart. A reasonable share of her attention is going to innovation—but we were surprised that it wasn't larger, since that's the most important part of her job. Business logistics get a lot of her attention, even though they're not meant to be Sally's major concern. Teamwork runs a distant third among her attention getters, followed by client and interpersonal issues.

The shades on Sally's chart indicate that she finds most of her work interesting. But almost every item on Sally's chart is plotted left of the axis line, indicating that

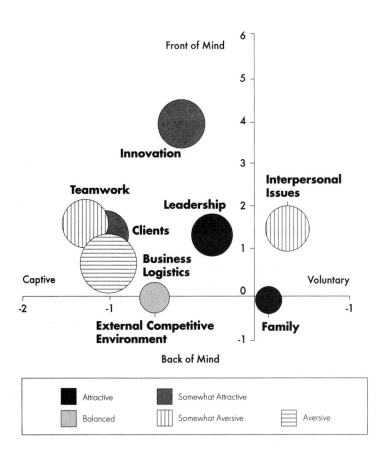

her attention to her work is captive—she's focusing because she feels she has to. And most of the items are in the front-of-mind area of the chart. This means that Sally hasn't been able to make parts of her job routine. She goes through her day paying close, conscious attention to almost everything, including items that really don't require—or deserve—such a large chunk of her expensive focus. People who keep everything in front-of-mind attention are easily overwhelmed, overworked, and overwrought. Based on this chart, we can conclude that Sally might need some help directing her attention to Floppy-Tech's most pressing corporate issues.

The AttentionScape is used in a number of ways: with leadership teams to understand their focus; with potential movie viewers to predict their likelihood of going to any given movie; and within companies to assess the "attention chain" throughout the organization. The charts are simple to create: the user compiles a list of attention items to rate, assesses how much of his or her or the team's total attention is paid to each item, and then vets out—through the use of analytical statements—the type of attention that is paid to each. While these charts are constructed with mathematical algorithms, the logic is quite simple, and you can map a theoretical AttentionScape without any numbers. (To walk through the process, go to www.attentionscape.net.)

Originally published in September–October 2000
Reprint R00505

The Successor's Dilemma

DAN CIAMPA AND MICHAEL WATKINS

Executive Summary

BOTCHED LEADERSHIP TRANSITIONS occur with alarming frequency—a fact that's laid bare regularly in the business pages of the nation's newspapers. The headlines trumpet the premature departures of designated successors—leaders such as Merrill Lynch's Herb M. Allison and AT&T's John Walter, who left their respective companies before they could claim the CEO's seat.

Dan Ciampa and Michael Watkins, who have counseled senior executives and successors through more than 100 leadership transitions in the past 25 years, point to the *successor's dilemma* as the dominant cause of failed leadership transition. The dilemma is an emotionally charged power struggle played out between the CEO and his would-be heir.

Ciampa and Watkins describe the way the problem builds on both sides of the desk—the CEO's fear of giving up control versus the designated successor's need to enact the changes expected of him and prove himself to the board. They cite anecdotal evidence and their own research to suggest that this complex psychological dynamic leads CEO-successor relations astray and can block the successor's path to the top spot.

But the authors also offer four ways for the would-be heir to overcome the successor's dilemma. These include gauging the CEO's readiness to leave before accepting the number two spot, maintaining regular communication with the CEO despite ever-present obstacles, such as travel and business schedules, and developing and using a *balanced personal advice network* to help navigate the shift in power.

The authors stress that defusing the problem is the responsibility of the successor, not the CEO. The reason is simple: the successor has the most to lose.

A WELL-REGARDED CEO approaches retirement age. He knows it is only responsible to designate a successor, and the board agrees wholeheartedly. Together, they screen internal candidates but decide that none possesses all the skills necessary to propel the company forward. Soon, a bright star is hired from outside the company—with the assurance that if he performs well, he will ascend to the top spot in two or three years.

At first the successor dazzles. He launches impressive strategic initiatives, some that yield surprisingly fast results, and he deploys managerial practices that get work done more effectively than ever. The CEO and the board congratulate themselves for their wise choice. Slowly but surely, however, the star's brilliance begins to dim. His take-charge approach starts to alienate the CEO and key members of the senior management team. Then it offends them outright. Soon, his initiatives are resisted, and some are even blocked altogether.

The designated successor grows frustrated, even angry. In his gut, he knows what is going on: the CEO is having trouble letting go of his job. He's not ready to give up control of the company he has toiled to build. Still, the board expects the designated successor to post impressive results, and the successor himself knows he must make organizational and strategic changes to prepare the company for the time when he will lead it. But without support from the CEO and his team, how can he take charge? The successor's hands are tied. If he pushes too hard, he alienates the CEO; if he doesn't push hard enough, his performance won't warrant a promotion to the top spot.

Thus the stage is set for the *successor's dilemma,* a seemingly intractable set of circumstances that has entangled leaders for as long as there have been organizations. Indeed, the drama of leadership succession is a timeless part of the human condition—think of the Biblical story of Saul and David and Shakespeare's King Lear. In both cases, the kings eventually found themselves unable to let go after choosing someone to succeed them. In modern times and organizations, the succession story plays out with similar themes. For the would-be leader, succession is a time of great excitement and promise, the culmination of a long and arduous climb to the top. For the incumbent leader, succession is a time to confront the passage of time, the end of a career, and even mortality itself. It is no wonder that relationships between successors and those they hope to replace are so fraught with emotion.

The successor's dilemma presents a pair of damning alternatives. If a CEO resists passing the torch, his would-be successor can wage open war to win the top job—but that can get ugly and rarely works. Or the successor can resign—a "solution" that can seriously damage the successor's reputation and his wallet. He may walk away relatively unscathed, but a high-profile failure might make second chances hard to come by.

The successor's dilemma is exacerbated by the fact that few people in an organization can help the successor and the CEO work out their crisis. Most boards of directors drop out of sight once the successor is hired; they check in only periodically. Similarly, most human resources executives don't play a mitigating role, primarily because few of them are the kind of trusted advisers necessary to negotiate a peace treaty between the CEO and his designated successor. Thus the CEO and his would-be heir are on their own to overcome, or be overcome by, the successor's dilemma. It's the latter that happens most often.

But the successor's dilemma itself can be overcome. Four practices can allay, and even prevent, the problem. Before he accepts the number two position, the successor can learn as much as possible about the CEO to assess his emotional readiness to leave his position. The successor can make it a top priority to maintain regular communication with the CEO. He can also develop and utilize a *balanced personal advice network* to help navigate the strategic and personal minefields of the leadership change. And, finally, he can stay focused on the endgame—that is, on his professional goals, not the emotional traps that surround them.

The successor must be responsible for managing the dilemma, because it is he who has the most to lose. The CEO's legacy might be tainted by conflict with his would-be heir, particularly if it is covered by the media. The board may take a hit to its credibility, having bungled one of its primary jobs. And many employees stand to suffer if the CEO and the successor battle it out. But no one pays the price of the successor's dilemma quite like the successor himself. He must own the problem—and its solution.

The Succession Minefield

Botched leadership transitions occur with alarming frequency. John Walter was installed as president of AT&T in October 1996—and was gone within nine months. Disney put Michael Ovitz in place as president in August 1995; he departed late the next year when his relationship with chairman Michael Eisner soured. A likely heir apparent at Citigroup, Jamie Dimon, exited in 1998. And just this past summer, Merrill Lynch president and chief operating officer Herb M. Allison resigned before claiming the top leadership position many thought was his.

The evidence isn't just anecdotal, however. Looking at records from 1992 for thousands of publicly traded companies, we identified 94 that had appointed a new person to the position of chief operating officer that year. Of those 94 would-be CEOs, 35 were brought in from outside the organization. Five years later, 22 of those executives had left the company before being promoted and four were still in their original position—fully 75% had not made it to the top as expected. (This article focuses on the transitions of successors hired from the outside. For a brief discussion of internal successions, see "It's Different from the Inside" at the end of this article.)

Just as it would be impossible to link every failed marriage to a single phenomenon, it's impossible to attribute every failed leadership transition to the successor's dilemma. But our research and experience strongly suggest that it is, by far, the dominant driver of failed successions. Indeed, one of us has served as an adviser to CEOs and their would-be successors during more than 100 transitions in the past 25 years. In every one of those cases, the successor's dilemma was at work, wreaking its unique brand of personal and organizational havoc.

An All-Too-Human Dynamic

The dynamics of the successor's dilemma can begin long before the successor sets foot in his new office. Even if a company is successful, the board typically wants to bring in a second in command who can meet an *anticipated* challenge—an emerging technology, for example. That is why the board and the CEO often agree that they must bring in a so-called "change agent" to eventually run the organization. When the search produces such a leader, the board makes it clear that great things are expected of the designated successor—and fast.

And so the new successor plunges in to learn about products, markets, and internal processes. Even for executives with years of experience, the learning curve can be quite steep in the early months; after all, no two companies are identical. At the same time, the successor must learn to operate in an unfamiliar corporate culture. Indeed, he must make a new political system work to his advantage. That means building credibility with people who now report to him—some of whom expected to be named to the job he was hired to fill. As one executive told us about his early days in the successor's position, "I thought I was pretty prepared coming into the job because of my background in finance and because I was head of marketing [at my former company]. Those were the areas that needed attention here, too. But I didn't count on the culture being so different. The marketing issues were tough enough, but I had to get people to think differently to get things done faster, and to get them to work across departments and functions. That was just brand new to them."

In the midst of this intense learning period, the successor must also try to build a relationship with the person he hopes to replace, a process that is riddled with pitfalls. Because he's coming from the outside, the successor barely knows the CEO and therefore enters the relationship gingerly. The successor usually avoids challenging the CEO even when he disagrees with him. That reticence is understandable, but it can plant the seeds of trouble. Take the case of the executive who joined a large financial services company as chief operating officer and expected to take over in three years when the chairman retired. The chairman had helped shape the industry, had founded the industry association, and had trained several executives who went on to become successful CEOs at other companies. He wasn't an arrogant person, but the chairman's reputation made him an intimidating figure.

The financial services company was in good shape but had room to improve. It needed to improve the efficiency of its business operations in order to keep costs down. The new successor quickly spotted ways to do so, but he didn't know how to tell the chairman without sounding disrespectful. In fact, he kept his opinions to himself and publicly supported the chairman's status quo approach to the business. In this case, the board recognized the bind the COO was in and helped him resolve it. Much more often, the successor's silence can lead him to frustration and anger.

The CEO's View

If the successor is facing new and daunting challenges, so too is the CEO. Indeed, our experience and research indicate that he typically passes through three distinct phases after a successor is designated. In the first phase, he feels pleased with having "done his duty" by installing a replacement. That satisfaction can last several weeks or several months, depending on how quickly the successor moves to make changes.

When the successor starts shaking things up, however, the CEO enters the second phase—growing discomfort and gradual resistance. While he may be happy to have found a successor to whom he can entrust the company, the CEO soon discovers that the cost of a smooth transition is having to give up control. He is confronted with the reality of handing over important decisions to someone who can certainly run the organization well enough but who has a different style and different priorities. The CEO must face up to the fact that his successor will run the company differently—and that just *feels* wrong. He still wants the transition to go forward and tries to hide his defensive reactions, at least initially. But that doesn't make his feelings less intense.

As the CEO struggles to retain some control, he also discovers that having a successor requires him to share the limelight in his interactions with the board, stock market analysts, and the press. Accepting that shift requires a level of humility that most CEOs are not known for. One CEO we observed relished his high profile. Tensions quickly developed when he hired a COO who was an aggressive change agent. Matters came to a head when the COO was on a business trip. The CEO used the opportunity to change reporting relationships: he assigned the head of IT to report to the chief financial officer, who reported to the CEO. Even though the move stirred up tension within the company, it helped the CEO retain the sense that he was the one in charge.

Also in the second phase, chief executives begin to confront the question of what to do once they retire. For people who have devoted every thought and energy to the job for many years—and who delight in their identity as CEO—this can be a difficult, even terrifying, consideration. Research on retiring CEOs points out that many chief executives of successful companies are anointed heroes by grateful employees or investors. As a result, they come to believe not

As the CEO feels his power in eclipse, the successor's impulse is to push for more and deeper change.

only that they deserve such praise but also that they are indispensable to the ongoing success of the enterprise.[1] As they contemplate leaving, their heroic self-concept revolts. They cannot live without the company that defines them, and they believe that the company cannot live without them.

In this context, many CEOs start to ponder the meaning and extent of their legacy. They ask themselves what they will be remembered for—and many realize that it might be overshadowed, or perhaps even diminished, by what the new leader is trying to do. For instance, one CEO had spent much of his career building his company's manufacturing capabilities; under the CEO's leadership, the company had bought or built 15 plants across the United States. His successor, he knew, would likely sell them all to focus the company more on providing services. Similarly, another CEO considered his greatest accomplishment at his company to be the creation of a culture in which employees cared for and respected one another. In the name of improving financial results, his successor would surely dismantle it, the CEO realized, to install a more performance-driven atmosphere. Rationally, both CEOs knew their successors had to make the changes; indeed, they had endorsed those changes themselves. But that didn't stop their feelings of sadness and resentment about the new plans. A legacy is a deeply painful thing to lose, and emotions can take over.

As the CEO feels his power in eclipse, the successor's impulse is to push for more and deeper change. With a few successful initiatives under his belt, he calls more openly for renewal and reinvention, and he articulates more widely his vision for the company. That only exacerbates the CEO's already threatened sense of identity and control, and he digs in his heels. The two "sides" enter into more open conflict, and communication between them falls off precipitously. Indeed, it is at about this time that phase three—active resistance—begins to emerge.

Right around the time the successor should be getting ready to move up, he is facing the fact that the CEO wants him to leave.

What often happens next is a turning point from which there is no easy return. The CEO calls for support from his troops—mostly members of his senior team. Many are willing accomplices. They are feeling overwhelmed by the successor's changes and have strong personal ties to the CEO. As soon as the CEO shows disagreement with the successor's style or direction, even subtly, the senior team feels free to operate around or without the designated successor—for example, going directly to the CEO with ideas or plans.

The dynamic spirals downward from there. Thinking he has no other alternative, the successor continues to pursue his change agenda to win the board's approval. In fact, in many cases he tries harder than ever to post impressive results. Ironically, if the successor succeeds, the CEO feels even more threatened, which causes the relationship to deteriorate further. If he doesn't succeed, the CEO points to that as evidence that the successor doesn't deserve the top job. In either case, right around the time the successor should be getting ready to move up, he is facing the fact that the CEO wants him to leave. In most of those cases, after a period of awkward or painful thrashing about on both sides, the successor does leave.

Meeting the Challenge

Leadership transitions are high-stakes situations, but the fact is, most people aren't prepared to meet them. That's not surprising. Few executives go through more than one high-level leadership change in their lifetime. The first step toward becoming prepared is understanding the dynamic that undergirds a changing of the guard. Indeed, just knowing that a psychological drama is at work is useful. But such understanding is not sufficient—action is. And that action, as we noted, is the successor's responsibility. Virtually every number two executive that we have observed and worked with makes the same point: don't expect anyone to solve this problem for you, including the CEO. As one successor who overcame a difficult transition said, "If my daughter were going through this, I would tell her that the way to increase the likelihood of making a successful transition is to never assume that anyone else cares as much about your success as you do. You have to take on the process yourself."

That process, we have found, includes the following practices:

Learn as much as possible about the CEO, professionally and personally, before signing on. The successor can help himself by doing his homework before taking the job. As he learns about the company, he should make it a point to learn, too, about the CEO's career and personality and how he might deal with the reality of his own retirement. That requires delicate investigation, and solid answers can't be guaranteed. Nevertheless, the executive search firm should be able to shed light on the CEO's state of mind, and the successor might also gather relevant information from interviews with board members who know the CEO well.

An executive can also discuss the transition process with the CEO himself—making sure, of course, not to suggest that he is anxious for the CEO to step aside quickly. In such a dialogue, a successor candidate can get a sense of the CEO's views on leadership transitions by asking questions about the CEO's own shift to power. Was it smooth? Was there an adviser involved? Is that person still available? What was the role of the board? The information uncovered in such a diagnostic process may not stop a successor from walking into a difficult situation, but at least he will be more prepared for the challenges he meets along the way.

Maintain regular communication with the CEO. As simple as it sounds, talk is a powerful antidote to the successor's dilemma. If a successor finds ways to make sure he and the CEO are in near constant conversations, he has gone far to prevent the misunderstandings and missed cues of the fragile leadership-in-transition dynamic. Unfortunately, it is easy for the successor and CEO *not* to talk. Both are busy, usually with different initiatives, and both travel. Both executives also have different sets of colleagues and friends within and outside the organization, which makes impromptu conversations less common.

To overcome those obstacles, the successor must seize every opportunity to spend time with the CEO. The successor can—and should—travel with the CEO to visit business plants or customers. He should take the lead in setting up regular meetings with the CEO to review the business—and he should go into those sessions with more questions than assertions. Meetings work better when they are dialogues, not reports.

The successor also might make it a point to talk to the CEO before announcing a major decision, such as an organizational change or an alliance. In fact, the most savvy successors use such meetings to test their ideas and solicit the CEO's input. That's good for the business and great for the relationship. Which leads to another point: communication between the successor and the CEO is good in and of itself, but it's even more effective when the successor makes sure that his words communicate sincere respect for the CEO. If overdone, respect can sound obsequious, but when a successor praises his boss occasionally and genuinely, it sets a tone that goes far toward defusing the tensions of the successor's dilemma.

Assemble and frequently confer with a balanced personal advice network. Because few companies have built-in systems to facilitate leadership transitions, successors must create their own network of advisers to help them navigate this minefield. The best networks for this purpose include some people who can offer advice on strategy or operations, and others who can offer counsel on the political realities of a company going through an operational change and a leadership handoff. Balanced personal advice networks should be composed of a judicious mix of external and internal advisers. External advisers should be drawn from the successor's mentors, colleagues, and friends outside the company; they should have only his interests at heart. Internal advisers should have the requisite technical knowledge and deep insight of the company's operations, history, politics, and culture.

The usefulness of a balanced personal advice network can be seen in the case of one successor who found that the culture of the company he had joined stood firmly in the way of his plans for fast-paced change. The company's customer service was poor, and the designated successor quickly determined the reason. "We never delivered to our customers on time because the production schedule was based on relationships, not procedures," he recalled. "If a product manager was launching a new product and needed the plant manager to change the schedule, they'd negotiate it at the card game on Friday night or over a beer. It would never get done at a production meeting. So people who didn't know how to play the game were at a real disadvantage, and our costs and schedule in the plant were a mess." The successor knew he couldn't turn to the CEO for help. "He had helped to create that culture," he explained.

The successor sought advice from two people. One was a consultant who had previously worked with the company on improving its operations and its culture.

The consultant was respected by managers throughout the company and by the CEO. The second person was his retired boss and mentor, who understood production supply problems and was creative in solving them. Just as important, his former boss cared deeply about the successor's career.

Over the next few weeks, the consultant met with a cross section of people who were involved in product supply, mapped the decision-making processes, and calculated the costs of the current way of operating. He also met with the successor and the successor's former boss to review his findings. Together, the three formulated and implemented a strategy that resulted in major improvements in customer service. Best of all, they did so without ruffling too many feathers—one of the prime virtues of a balanced personal advice network.

A final way in which a balanced personal advice network can be used is in mediation. A board member, an outside adviser, or a senior staff member can bring the successor and CEO together if he has the trust of both parties and if he has no vested interest except in wanting to see a positive resolution. Such a person might also be able to reason with the CEO in a way that the second in command cannot. (For an example of such facilitation, see "A Succession Saved from the Brink" at the end of this article.)

Stay focused on the endgame. Because of the intensity of emotions and competitive spirit of many successors, they may consider a disagreement with the CEO as a contest to be won. They temporarily lose sight of their ultimate goal: to move to the top and lead the company forward. One successor who failed to make the transition to the top slot lamented afterwards, "I had decided early on what I wanted before any of my friends did—the kind of job and the sort of place I wanted to work at. When I got the successor's job, it was like I had gone to heaven. It was all right there." Then, he recalled, "I got drawn into a battle that I never intended to fight. I let myself get distracted by my feelings and pride, and I took my eye off the real goal." This leader failed to manage his emotions. He let the successor's dilemma get the best of him. Scrambling toward his goal, he didn't know when to pull back or how to do it gracefully. Leaders must be able to do both of those things to manage the successor's dilemma.

One way for the successor to keep his emotions in check is to practice empathy and focus on what the CEO is going through rather than on his own experience. One designated successor embroiled in a difficult transition came to understand what his boss was experiencing, with some help from his wife and two board members. They helped him see that the CEO's actions, such as overruling the successor's decisions and taking over his meetings, didn't prove that he had changed his mind about retiring. Rather they showed that the CEO was struggling with losing the position that gave him his identity. The successor's wife put it most directly by saying, "This is not about you. [The CEO] is not thinking about you at all as he's doing these things. It's all about him."

Perhaps the hardest part of managing the successor's dilemma is allowing the CEO himself to save face. It can also be the most critical part. Take the case mentioned earlier in this article about the CEO who changed reporting duties while his successor was away. At first, the COO was angry when he returned from his trip. But he soon realized this was not a battle to pick. The CEO only wanted to show the organization he was still boss. The successor quietly met with the chief financial officer, and together they decided they would both work with the head of IT. "I decided that I could still get the changes I wanted in IT," the successor recalled, "and that the only reason to make an issue about it was my ego." He let the CEO's pride win instead, and he went on to land the top job 18 months later.

A Timeless Drama

The poignant and often painful drama of succession is ages old. As one person rises to new heights, another must fall, or at least step back from the spotlight. Thus succession forces its players to confront the hard and eternal human questions of power and identity. And they must do so with many eyes on them, including the media, their colleagues, and their families. But the hardest audience the characters in the succession drama must face are themselves and each other.

Yet leadership transitions can be managed in ways that make success more likely. The successor can prepare for the challenge before joining the organization. Once he does that, he can work assiduously to create a good relationship with the incumbent leader. He can also draw on the outside help of advisers. In the end, the success or failure of a leadership transition belongs to the successor, and it always will.

Notes

1. Jeffrey A. Sonnenfeld, *The Hero's Farewell* (Oxford University Press, 1988).

It's Different from the Inside

THE SUCCESSOR'S DILEMMA is clearly a tough challenge for executives coming from outside the company.
But what about executives moving up from inside the
business? They're better off, according to our research.
We found that about half of the internal successors in our
study were promoted to CEO within five years compared with about a quarter of the successors who had
been hired from the outside.

Without question, internal CEO candidates have an
edge because they already understand the organization's culture and politics and have established relationships with the CEO and other senior managers. But the
fact that half aren't successful in becoming CEOs indicates they still face substantial challenges:

- They must **recast their relationships** within the organization
as they become the boss to former coworkers and super-
visors. Colleagues who were passed over for the successor's job often present the most difficulty; they resist the
new leader's direction much more than they would resist
directives from someone brought in from the outside.

- They must **modify people's expectations** of them. The
organization knows the insider as he was. But once he is
promoted and given a mandate for change, the successor must introduce new ways of operating the business,
hold people to higher standards, and spend time with
new stakeholders, such as the board.

- They must **rebuild the top team** or create a new one,
either by hiring from the outside or by moving people up
from within the organization. While the successor almost
certainly won't move people around much during the

transition itself, he will have to deal carefully with colleagues who are jockeying for position and trying to secure their jobs in anticipation of his takeover.

Inside and outside successors do share one challenge. Both must deal with the strong emotions—and inevitable resistance—of the CEO. Just because the successor comes from within the company, that doesn't mean the CEO will let go more easily. Nor does the successor's insider status mean that he won't want to make his own bold mark during the transition period. If the two individuals had any problems before the transition, those conflicts will be accentuated now. If the two executives had no problems, some are sure to develop—and will demand careful attention.

A Succession Saved from the Brink

THE STORY OF BILL AND HOWARD begins like a leadership transition bound to fail. It didn't. Bill, a talented executive brought in to succeed Howard as CEO of a large manufacturing company, used several simple but highly effective practices to stop the successor's dilemma in its well-worn tracks.

Bill and Howard's problems began about two years after Bill joined the company as president of international operations. Bill hadn't been given an outright guarantee that he would make it to the top position, but he had received strong assurances. Howard, he was told, had agreed with the board that he would retire in three years. If all went well, the CEO's post was Bill's.

Both Howard and the board had exhorted Bill to get international operations back on track. The division had been strong in the past, but performance had suffered as aggressive competitors made inroads. To make matters worse, two recent product launches had failed, and costs were rising. Despite those problems, the company's new strategic plan called for double-digit growth outside the United States. It was up to Bill to achieve that.

Bill got off to a good start, and within a year and a half he was making solid improvements. He had accelerated product launches, cut manufacturing costs, and streamlined distribution. Market share rebounded, and profits climbed. Bill was on a roll, and the financial community took notice.

Along the way, Bill kept Howard informed of his actions and saw no indication that he disagreed. But just as Bill began to post good results, his relationship with Howard started to sour. In year-end reviews, Howard praised Bill publicly for what he had accomplished. But both men could feel a chill. One obvious reason was that they simply did not spend any time together. Bill's international travel prevented it. But there were other problems, too.

Bill was feeling increasingly restless. When would the board and Howard start talking about succession? Surely, he thought, he had earned the top job by now. Meanwhile, Howard was developing cold feet. He was only 64 and in good health. Bill had been with the company for less than two years. Now that the international division was back on track, why shouldn't he remain and lead the company he had spent close to a decade building? These are the best of times, Howard told himself, so why leave now?

After a few small snubs from Howard, Bill considered asking him to talk things over but decided to wait. For one thing, he reasoned, if Howard thought that he was trying to push him out prematurely, a meeting might back-fire. Anyway, he decided, it was up to Howard to initiate a dialogue. Bill concluded that his best course was to keep posting great results.

In the next few months, Bill accelerated his pace. He cut costs again in the plants and entered into a major dis-tribution alliance—without consulting Howard. The agree-ment meant that the international division would need to hit more challenging targets than ever, but Bill believed that the pact's benefits far outweighed the temporary stress it might cause. He also knew the deal would catch the attention of the board, who might then advocate for his promotion.

The deal did get attention, but it also angered Howard, and the CEO's active resistance began. He started telling other executives that Bill was taking too much cost out of the plants and that the new alliance was full of booby traps. Howard grumbled to himself about being left out of the loop and upstaged. He was still CEO, wasn't he?

It soon became apparent that Bill's new distribution alliance was a success. It increased revenues, and when paired with the cost cutting, boosted profits. The board was delighted; they decided that Bill had earned the right to be named chief operating officer and to be nomi-nated to a board seat, publicly putting him in line to suc-ceed Howard.

Over the next weeks, Howard went from remote to icy. He never congratulated Bill on his promotion and never mentioned the board position at all. Howard con-tinued to make all the corporate decisions and said noth-ing about a handoff. Bill became increasingly worried that Howard had changed his mind about retirement and that he'd been parked in a job with no power.

Tensions hit a peak when a national business magazine wanted to spotlight the company and wanted to put Bill on its cover. Howard vetoed it.

Now Bill was angry. His first impulse was to leave; he had gotten several calls about attractive management positions in larger companies. At the same time, he wanted to complete what he had started in a company he had come to like. So he turned to two key people in his personal advice network—his wife and a trusted outside adviser. Bill accepted the chance to step back, count to ten, and more rationally decide on the best course of action.

He consulted several board members confidentially. Howard would have been threatened if he had known about the meetings, but it was worth the risk to Bill. He wanted to affirm the board's commitment to Howard's retirement—and to Bill as the next CEO.

Bill then approached Cliff, the company's chief financial officer, whom he had come to trust. His appeal to this internal adviser—who also was respected by Howard—is what helped this successor story have a happy ending. Cliff opened Bill's eyes to what Howard was going through—his unease about losing his identity as CEO and his fear that his legacy might be eclipsed. "Bill, we're talking about his emotions here. This has nothing to do with your performance," Cliff told him. "Howard needs an exit plan, one that lets him leave gracefully and go to something that he's excited about. He's keeping all this inside because he's used to being the one with the answers."

As he and Cliff talked, Bill realized that a smooth transition was as important to his success as any of his strategic or operational accomplishments. Bill knew that the managers whose support he needed in order to be a successful CEO were loyal to Howard. He couldn't appear to be forcing Howard out. Moreover, Bill respected Howard. He wanted to see him leave with the credit he deserved. He knew he had to speak with Howard and begin to work toward a transition that made sense to both of them. Cliff agreed to facilitate the discussion.

The first meeting lasted six hours. The executives began by focusing on the distribution alliance and on Howard's anger at not being consulted about it, but the discussion quickly moved to deeper issues in the relationship. Although the meeting was awkward for both leaders, they were able to share their concerns with help from Cliff. Howard expressed his misgivings about leaving the company and going into retirement. Bill assured Howard he had no intention of rushing him from his post. By the end of the session, the successor and his boss agreed to meet in person every two weeks and have monthly checkup sessions with Cliff present.

One year later, Bill did indeed succeed Howard in a smooth leadership transition that almost got away.

Originally published in November–December 1999
Reprint 99604

The Rise and Fall of the J. Peterman Company

JOHN PETERMAN

Executive Summary

IN 1987, JOHN PETERMAN started the J. Peterman
Company with a $500 investment and a $20,000 unsecured loan. What began with an ad in the *New Yorker*
and a single product prospered for years. But in 1998,
the company slid harrowingly into bankruptcy proceed-
ings. What happened?

As Peterman tells it, it all started with a trip he took to
Jackson Hole, Wyoming, where he bought a coat. It
was a long, sweeping cowboy duster, and he liked the
way wearing it made him feel. He suspected that other
people would like to buy something that made them feel
romantic and individualistic, too. He was right. With Don
Staley writing the copy, Peterman issued the first catalog
in 1988. It contained just seven items. By 1989, the company did $4.8 million in sales; by 1990, that figure had
grown to $19.8 million.

But the business model was always implicit—a mistake. They should have developed a precise mission statement. In hindsight, Peterman says, it would have been easy. The business concept could have been summed up in six words: unique, authentic, romantic, journey, wondrous, and excellent. The most successful items evoked all of those things.

The business grew, and as more items were added to the catalog and their retail stores expanded, everyone in the company had difficulty focusing. Rapid expansion in the late 1990s brought more staff, more backers, more risk, more rules, and less focus. Time ran out when a cash-flow crisis ultimately squeezed the life out of the company. Looking back, Peterman draws a number of transferable lessons about creating a dream and building a culture, and about the nature of trust and control in a growing organization.

T HERE COMES A TIME IN THE life of a growing business when you, as its founder and top manager, realize that the company has taken on a momentum of its own. You influence it, certainly, but more and more you are swept along by it. I hit that point in 1996. I created the J. Peterman Company on a $500 investment and $20,000 borrowed, unsecured. I made the company grow. I gave it momentum. And then I began to recognize that it had gained a momentum of its own. I watched it hit its stride—and then I watched it stumble and fall. J. Peterman went into Chapter 11 on January 25, 1999, and has been purchased by Paul Harris Stores, to reemerge as what, I'm not sure. I am no longer associated with it.

Now I'm in a transition period. I'm saddened by the loss of J. Peterman. (I mean that quite literally. Ironically, John Peterman is J. Peterman, and J. Peterman is John Peterman, but I no longer own the J. Peterman name.) And I've been operating—living—under significant pressure. Going through a bankruptcy is unmercifully stressful. It's very difficult—even in the aftermath—to focus on the future. I am jumping back on the horse; it's in my genes. To tell the truth, though, deciding which horse to jump on hasn't been easy. Figuring out a strategy—deciding which direction I want to go in as a person and as an entrepreneur—has been hard. Particularly since I have to think about it this time. There wasn't a huge amount of strategizing involved in creating the J. Peterman catalog business. It was intuitive, it fit, it felt right. Any new project I take on must also feel right, but it must have a considered strategy as well. Sadly, that may mean I'll never allow myself quite the freedom and spontaneity I enjoyed for a time with the J. Peterman Company. But I feel that's the right way to move forward.

I'm getting ahead of myself. I'll go back to the beginning. I didn't sit down and say, "I'm going to build an organization with *this* kind of culture aimed at attracting *that* kind of customer." I knew what kind of culture I enjoyed working in; I strongly suspected that there were people who would respond to a company marketing romance and individuality. But the company was born, as it were, with my own purchase of a cowboy duster.

I bought the coat during a trip to Jackson Hole, Wyoming, because I liked it—it said something about me that I wanted said. It said that I don't need to wear something with a logo to show people who I am. It was romantic, different. I found when I wore it, strangers seemed to give me approving glances. In airports, people would try to meet my eye as I walked by them. And I thought, "I like the way this feels; I wonder if there are others who would appreciate the feeling as well."

Armed with that very unscientific research, my friend Don Staley and I decided to run an ad in the local Lexington, Kentucky, paper and see what we could sell. We thought that we would try writing about the way I felt wearing the duster—that we would try to create the context and see if that appealed to anyone. Well, we sold one. To my accountant's secretary, so it didn't really count. But, we thought, we'll just try one more time. So we ran some more ads, searching for the people we thought might be out there. We hit pay dirt with the ad we ran in the *New Yorker*. We sold 60 or 70 coats, and the J. Peterman Company was up and running.

It was a stressful time. I would buy dusters on 30-day terms, secure the ad space, and then use the money from the sales to pay for the ad. But then I had to run another ad to get the money to pay for the dusters. It worked in a cycle, and a few cycles into it, I realized that I couldn't afford to get out of the business; I owed so much money. Survival is a great motivator, and we knew that we were hitting a significant chord with the public, so we created the catalog and continued to push. Our first *Owner's Manual* catalog, with black-and-white drawings and that same romantic copy—which was to become our trademark—went out in the fall of 1988. It had seven items in it, including the duster. We mailed our first color book the following spring.

We made the cheese downstairs and ran J. Peterman upstairs in two rooms.

By the end of the first year, we had about three full-time people and three or four part-time people working with us—none of them making much money. My wife, Audrey, who was in charge of the whole back end, was getting paid (not much). I wasn't. But even with a staff, I didn't spend time thinking about the organization I was creating. I was too busy. In the beginning, I was maintaining myself by running a specialty-foods consultancy, along with a regional business that made and distributed Hall's BeerCheese, which had limited growth potential. All three businesses were located in one very old building; we made the cheese downstairs and ran J. Peterman upstairs in two rooms. One room was full of dusters and such, and the other had three desks and, believe it or not, a potbellied stove we used for heat. We were staying just ahead of the curve financially—selling stuff, paying the printer, sending out the catalog, selling stuff.

I was also looking for capital. I contacted 100 venture capitalists initially and was turned down by every single one. They would look at my very crude and rudimentary business plan and say, "Tell us about your experience in the catalog business."

And I would say, "I don't have any."

And they would say, "Well, tell us about your experience in the apparel business."

And I would say, "I don't have any."

And they would say, "Well, you'll have to go look for your money someplace else."

I had some near misses with several venture capitalists—one we came very close to finalizing a deal with before it fell through. (I had to sweet-talk the printer into running our catalog that cycle.) And then in 1989 we were approached by Hambro America. A man named Edwin Goodman called me and said something like, "We've seen your ad in the *New Yorker*, and we're kind of intrigued—thought maybe you would be looking for capital." And I said with barely contained excitement, "Possibly." The deal was done in three weeks.

We had come up with a very engaging concept for a business. We were getting a tremendously high response rate from prospects. Virtually every book we mailed had a very high response rate. In 1989, we did $4.8 million in sales, and in 1990, we did $19.8 million. Our staff grew even faster. We went from 15 people in 1989 to probably 75 or 80 in 1990, and we were all working well together toward a common, if unstated, goal. The road ahead looked exciting.

In the face of success, it's easy to assume that people joining the team know what the game is.

We had also, without realizing it, planted the seeds for serious problems later on. All the thinking about the brand, the niche, the target market—it was intuitive for a very long time. I wish now that we'd written down our ideas, our concept—in detail—at the start. It was a long time before we put anything into words in that way, and by then I think it was too late. The theory of our business was in my head and in Don's head (as creative director, he concentrated on writing and producing the catalogs), and until 1996, we took the time to make sure that it was also in the heads of everyone on staff. But in 1997, when we laid our plans for retail expansion and we had to recruit many more people quickly, it got lost. In the face of success and rapid growth, it's easy to assume that people joining the team know what the game is. Failing to make sure that everyone knows what you stand for and why—that can come right back and ambush you much sooner than you realize.

We did always have one thing in writing, a general philosophy, in our catalog. It was, "People want to live

life the way they wish they were." The problem was that
such a philosophy, so broadly stated, didn't give our
employees nearly enough guidance. We should have
developed a precise mission statement, or something
along those lines.

It's easy for me to do that now. In fact, I can sum up
the concept of the business in six words: "unique,"
"authentic," "romantic," "journey," "wondrous," and
"excellent." The items we sold—the ones that were most
successful—were all of those things. The duster, for
example. It would definitely have been unusual on the
Upper East Side. At the same time, though, it wasn't con-
trived; it certainly wouldn't have been unusual on a
ranch. It evoked a sense of romance; cowboys are romantic figures. Worn outside the context of a ranch, it
implied that the wearer was on a journey, intellectually
and emotionally. With that implication came a certain
sense of wonder. And its quality was excellent. At one
point early on, in fact, we lost the supplier for the duster,
so I cut up one of the coats, took out all the stitching,
sourced 22 different components, and found a manufacturer to produce it. That duster embodied the six words;
it *was* the company. There was never a question about
replacing it even with a similar product, though we were,
for a time, up against the wall.

At any rate, when we matched our products with
those six words, we were successful. The duster, the J.
Peterman shirt (a colonial style—99% Thomas Jefferson,
1% Peterman), even the items we associated with classic
movies—all met the criteria. When we strayed from the
six words, we faltered. Toward the end of the company,
we were developing 2,000 new products a year. There is
just no way to generate 2,000 products that are truly
romantic, unique, and authentic.

Some people have questioned whether we were true to our concept by pursuing and selling the props from the movie *Titanic*, very late in the company's life. We were. The sinking of the actual ship *Titanic* during the Edwardian era was a terrible tragedy, but it was also a romantic story. (Tragedies often are.) The products were authentic movie props; we never led people to believe that the materials came off the ship, nor did we want them to think so. The connection we aimed to create for customers was with the movie, as well as with the actual event. What we were helping customers capture for themselves was the magic of Hollywood, along with the romance of the time and of the story.

Where we strayed from our concept was in selling reproductions of the "heart of the ocean" necklace worn by the heroine in the movie. The product did well, but selling it was a clear commercial decision. We shouldn't have. It was not authentic, it was tied too completely to the movie, and it appealed to an audience younger than our target 35 to 55 year olds. It was a costly success in terms of our brand's integrity. On the other hand, selling the "Kate Winslet dress," a reproduction of one of the costumes from the movie, was just fine. The dress was of the Edwardian period; it was something we might have carried even without the movie.

We were also true to our concept when we recreated the ambiance of the catalog in our retail stores. The problem with the retail stores was the pace of our expansion, not the decision to expand. But I'll get to that later.

I put a lot of time into thinking about how the retail stores could reflect the sentiment and tone of the writing in the catalog, and I think that time paid off. The trick was taking the catalog one step further. Inviting customers to my Grandmother's barn, actually.

When I was ten years old, I would go to my grand-mother's barn, open the door, and be transfixed. I could spend hours, days, summers there, exploring all the won-derful treasures. It was that sense of discovery that we aimed to re-create in the retail environment. And it worked. The full-price retail stores averaged over $500 per square foot in sales. The store in Grand Central Sta-tion did over $800 per square foot. A senior analyst from Goldman Sachs toured the store in the fall of 1998 and told us it was the freshest retail concept he'd seen in ten years.

Peterman on-line shopping was another story. I hadn't spent much time thinking about the potential of the Web, and I didn't really see the need to. I knew our Web site wasn't very exciting, but my focus was elsewhere. The Web certainly got my attention when we sold half a mil-lion dollars' worth of "heart of the ocean" necklaces in about six weeks. But before that, and afterwards, the site just puttered along. Since I left the J. Peterman Company, I have spent a great deal more time thinking about how retail can work, and should work, on the Internet. My next business, in fact, will be Web oriented. I don't know whether we missed an opportunity, large or small, by not devoting more attention to e-commerce at J. Peterman. But speculating about that now won't do anyone any good.

This seems like as good a place as any to mention *Seinfeld*. A lot of people have asked me about the J. Peter-man character on what was then the number one televi-sion show in America. In fact, a good many people have said that I had a blind spot where the Peterman charac-ter was concerned. That I missed an enormous opportu-nity to take advantage of the character and all the pub-licity. That I should have hired the actor who portrayed me, John O'Hurley, to represent the company. I don't think so. Certainly, we missed an opportunity to exploit the name recognition; most people who watched *Seinfeld* didn't realize that we were a real company or that J. Peterman was a real person. In retrospect, we might have done more with that. But changing our business to dovetail with the fictitious one on television would have been too much of a commercial move, and our business had been built around the idea of staying away from commercialism.

The first appearance of Peterman on Seinfeld *coincided with increases in the prices of paper and postage; my mind wasn't on television.*

I did review the scripts. After the first time O'Hurley appeared as me on the show, *Seinfeld*'s lawyers contacted me, and we agreed that I would sign off on the scripts in which my character had a part. And we did put an Elaine Bennes suit into our catalog, mostly as a way of winking at our customers. But I regret doing that. It was one of those little decisions that was slightly off point for our brand. The suit actually sold quite well. But it was a good suit—I think it would have sold well even if we had called it "Barbara's suit." The problem was that it was a tick in the wrong direction. It may have been an excellent suit, but it did not embody any of the other elements. It was not romantic or wondrous. It represented no sort of journey. And it was not authentic; it was tied to a TV show that was entirely fictional.

Seinfeld was a bit of a nonstarter for me overall. The first appearance of the J. Peterman character on the show in May 1995 coincided with a substantive increase in the prices of postage and paper. We posted a significant loss that year, and it was hard to take. So my mind wasn't on television; it was on retrenchment.

I was beginning to realize that we had reached the ceiling of potential for the *Owner's Manual* catalog. Our efforts at developing a home-hard-goods mail-order business were not progressing as I had hoped. I intuitively believed that our niche could be larger than a $65 million a year catalog business, so I started thinking about other ways to grow. Ultimately, we broke even in 1996. But even one flat year makes backers nervous, and I was starting to get some pressure from our investors (we had more by then) and from the bank (we had of course moved beyond the $20,000 by then, too) to "restart" the business. I also knew that we needed more capital, and none of our current investors was interested. That's when, at the end of 1996, I started considering rapid retail expansion and, along with it, the recruitment of name-brand managers. Investors want to see credentials on staff.

On paper, the expansion plans and their rate of implementation made sense. After all, only one in four people ever buy anything out of catalogs, but just about everyone shops in retail stores. Our existing retail stores—a full-price store in Lexington, Kentucky, and two outlets, one in Chattanooga, Tennessee, and another in Manchester, Vermont—were doing well.

Retail expansion also seemed to be a way to bring our finances in line. Our G&A expenses were getting too high. We broke even in 1996 because we cut back on advertising; we mailed fewer books and to more responsive customers. What we should have done in addition was cut back on the number of products we were offering.

We were adding items because we felt that the more items we offered, the more opportunity people would have to buy. There was ample evidence in general retail research to support that. So we continued the trend with our retail stores. But the more-is-better theory didn't work for us in practice. The more items we offered, whether through the catalog or through the stores, the less special—the less "Peterman"—each new item became. And we needed more staff to support the proliferation of products. It was the beginning of the end, but I didn't recognize it at the time.

All of which brings me to 1998, when we rolled out the very aggressive retail expansion. Let me be clear: left to my own devices, I wouldn't have moved that fast. But we had to expand aggressively to get the infusion of capital we wanted. In hindsight, maybe if I hadn't received the capital, I would have slashed the product line, as I should have. At the time, I didn't have the perspective to think along those lines. Expansion looked like survival to me.

Our many new products in turn created the need for many new business systems and an ever-expanding staff. It was too much change at once, and it was a recipe for disaster. I've covered the product proliferation problem. Now I'll tackle the staff and the systems problems. They're all related.

In the beginning, I didn't have the money to hire many people with "credentials." Most of our merchants rose through the ranks internally, working directly with me the whole way, and now I think that was just as well. It gave us the luxury of developing talent. Sure, your "insiders" have to have some talent to start with, but I found that it wasn't good to make the judgment call on that too early. The best people we had took a year to learn what the business was. To give you an example, when I brought in Paula Collins as a catch-all assistant back in 1990, her claim to fame was that she had been a secretary to a guy based in White Plains, New York, who exported nuts and bolts. Paula didn't exhibit a great deal of talent initially, but she did exhibit a great work ethic, a willingness to learn, and tremendous resiliency.

Very early on, Paula became the women's merchant. She would come in with a product, and I would say "that's not right; that's not the business we're in," and she would ask why, and we would go back and forth. She kept learning, kept trying to figure out what the business was about, and ultimately she developed into one of the best merchants in the industry.

The problem in 1997 and 1998 was that we were missing some very specific areas of expertise that I felt we needed to handle our retail expansion. And so we went outside for high-level employees to fill those gaps. Hiring at high levels from other companies isn't inherently a bad idea. I can't deny the need for new blood; outsiders bring fresh energy and perspective to the table, and we did hire very talented people. The idea of recruiting high-powered people with credentials, though, is that they can hit the road running. They never got the chance.

If you're changing systems—purchasing, computer, merchandising—you need high-level people who have been with the company awhile and know the business so they can keep it steady through the transition. If your systems are set, you can add high-level people from outside because they'll be able to start working within established guidelines. We were changing the systems and the people at the same time. The ground was moving; the newcomers never gained traction. What was needed was a carefully orchestrated transition period. We never slowed down long enough to allow for a transition period, much less manage it.

Doing what we did, the way we did it, caused problems on several levels. For one, our existing staff felt slighted. The people we brought in were in many cases making higher salaries for no good reason except that to hire them we had to meet what they were already making. And the spotlight was on the new folks. When decisions needed to be made, we paid more attention to the new staff than to the old-timers.

For another, the culture started to fray. We didn't have a hard time recruiting. It was well known that our culture was one of creativity and respect for people; there was no shortage of people who wanted to join that culture. But when you hire people from a culture that isn't respectful or from a culture that is very controlling, it's like bringing an abused dog into a friendly home. It takes time and a lot of patience and positive reinforcement for the dog to trust you—to know that every time you walk by you're not going to whack it.

When you don't have the time to offer continual positive reinforcement, the natural tendency is for the new people to slip back into old cultural habits. After all, that's what they know best. In the absence of constant reminders that they now have the authority to do *this*, and that the organization is structured so that they should feel free to do *that*, they'll re-create their old culture and set up boundaries between people, levels, and departments where none previously existed. We didn't have the time to keep reinforcing what we assumed was a rock-solid culture. And so the new team didn't have time to gel. There was friction; there was confusion.

We had had a culture in which every employee understood and recognized that every job was important, that everyone was a valued contributor. Culture can't be dictated; it must be absorbed over time. Until 1997 or so, we were giving newcomers the time they needed to absorb it.

I'll cite a brief example. From the beginning through 1996, I had breakfast each Friday with a different group of eight employees, randomly selected from all levels and areas of the company. The only rule at breakfast was, "There are no rules." People were encouraged to ask me any questions, personal or business related. We used the time simply to get to know one another. It was a small thing—it only took an hour a week—but it was tremendously important because it showed my employees that I cared about them. Well, things got too busy in 1997; I was out of the office a great deal trying to raise capital; I was working 12- or 14-hour days, seven days a week. The breakfasts got lost in the shuffle. That was telling.

Some postmortem critics have said that our open culture allowed too much freedom and that that freedom was a critical factor in the company's demise. Not true. I'll defend the culture we had in the early days—and tried to keep throughout the life of the company—to the death. We did not go bankrupt because of the culture.

Ultimately, the death of the J. Peterman Company was caused by a combination of things. We made mistakes, but we could have survived them. We were bombarded by external, out-of-our-control kinds of things, but we could have survived them. What we couldn't survive was our own mistakes coupled with the external, out-of-our-control kinds of things. We faced too many hurdles at once, and it all tumbled in on us.

For one thing, the business plan for 1998 was back-end loaded. That means we were counting on too many sales coming in during the last three months of the year. More seriously, that back-end loading was based on a direct-marketing fallacy. The theory was that if we offered customers more products—if we mailed a Peterman *Owner's Manual* to customers one week and followed up with a hard-goods book the next—we'd sell more stuff. We didn't. The catalogs competed with each

other for our customers' "Peterman dollars." We just
ended up doubling our marketing costs while leaving our
sales where they were. So while we built up our fixed
organization in anticipation of rapid growth in the next
year, those sales didn't materialize.

There are two theories of growth. One is that you let
organizational development lag behind business growth.
The danger with that approach is that you get too much
business, and then your company crumbles from within
because you don't have the staff to handle it. The other
theory is that you build the large organization to handle
the business you anticipate. That's what we did, at the
urging of the venture capitalists, and we ended up in a
liquidity crisis. I'll not disguise my feelings; I'm bitter.

Nothing seemed to work. In the midst of everything
else, we replaced our hard-goods book, *Peterman's Eye*,
with a new hard-goods book, *Peterman's Notebook*. The
Eye wasn't a loser, but it also wasn't hugely profitable,
and we thought we could do better. The problem was the
change cost too much, in time as well as money. It was
another bump in the road when we couldn't handle any
more bumps.

Offering more products meant not only confusing
customers and adding more staff to source items but
also adding more manufacturers and so forth, right
down the channel. To stay on top of things, we replaced
our old inventory-management system, but we never got
a handle on it. We did not manage inventory very well
toward the end, and that's a gracious comment.

And then our bank made a significant error, which
made our financial picture look much worse than it actually was. Even after they recognized the error, the people
handling our account didn't retreat from panic mode.
They started to squeeze us, in a legal way, though not to

my mind in an ethical way. They withheld an advance we had counted on; they refused to finance the inventory in our retail stores; they squeezed millions of dollars out of our fall line.

So there we were, faced with soft sales, fixed costs that were too high, too much inventory, and a lending squeeze. Add to that a breakdown at the printer, which delayed one of our catalogs by three weeks, which, in turn, aggravated a deal in the making that I had with another bank, and you've got a full-blown liquidity crisis.

Ultimately, the venture capitalists pulled out, we were unable to restructure, and you know the rest. There were several 11th-hour rescue attempts, but none panned out. I felt as though we were a plane going down. We were in a spiral at 30,000 feet, we leveled out at 20,000, went into a spiral again at 10,000, and then we had no altitude left. Our vendors got shafted and so did our employees, and I'm sorry.

Paul Harris bought the company—inventory, assets, the J. Peterman trademark—on March 5, 1999. End of story.

You know, the popular press has had a field day with Arnie Cohen, former president and chief operating officer of J. Crew, who joined us as president and COO in July of 1997. To some extent, they were justified. Arnie is a great salesman; he is very intelligent and has many good qualities. He had been involved in the company for almost a year as an adviser and consultant before he came on as president, and he had gained my complete confidence during that time. In retrospect, however, he wasn't as good an operator as I thought he was. He contributed to many of the transitional problems we had, in large part because he pushed the company to take on too many initiatives at once. He should have known better.

For my part, I should have listened more to my own intuition. I should have trusted myself—over anyone else—and I should have known when to say no.

It's tough to balance your own instincts as a founder and top manager with the desire to let the people you've hired do their thing. Managing managers wasn't something I set out to do; it was a job requirement that was incorporated by default into my position because my original idea for a business was a good one. But I think I drew out of this experience the skills to do it well; I believe that next time around I will know how to step back from the fray, assess things objectively, and make the right call. Next time, I'll get that right. That's not to say I'm in the market to lead just any company. I am, first and foremost, an entrepreneur. What drives me is the act of creating—the chase, if you will. But I know more now about what happens when an entrepreneur succeeds—more about the vicissitudes of the way. And I'm ready to try again.

Originally published in September–October 1999
Reprint 99507

Why Should Anyone Be Led by You?

ROBERT GOFFEE AND GARETH JONES

Executive Summary

WE ALL KNOW THAT LEADERS need vision and energy, but after an exhaustive review of the most influential theories on leadership—as well as workshops with thousands of leaders and aspiring leaders—the authors learned that great leaders also share four unexpected qualities.

The first quality of exceptional leaders is that they selectively reveal their weaknesses (weaknesses, not fatal flaws). Doing so lets employees see that they are approachable. It builds an atmosphere of trust and helps galvanize commitment.

The second quality of inspirational leaders is their heavy reliance on intuition to gauge the appropriate timing and course of their actions. Such leaders are good "situation sensors"—they can sense what's going on without having things spelled out for them.

Managing employees with "tough empathy" is the third quality of exceptional leadership. Tough empathy means giving people what they need, not what they want. Leaders must empathize passionately and realistically with employees, care intensely about the work they do, and be straightforward with them.

The fourth quality of top-notch leaders is that they capitalize on their differences. They use what's unique about themselves to create a social distance and to signal separateness, which in turn motivates employees to perform better.

All four qualities are necessary for inspirational leadership, but they cannot be used mechanically; they must be mixed and matched to meet the demands of particular situations. Most important, however, is that the qualities encourage authenticity among leaders. To be a true leader, the authors advise, "Be yourself—more—with skill."

IF YOU WANT TO SILENCE A ROOM of executives, try this small trick. Ask them, "Why would anyone want to be led by you?" We've asked just that question for the past ten years while consulting for dozens of companies in Europe and the United States. Without fail, the response is a sudden, stunned hush. All you can hear are knees knocking.

Executives have good reason to be scared. You can't do anything in business without followers, and followers in these "empowered" times are hard to find. So executives had better know what it takes to lead effectively— they must find ways to engage people and rouse their commitment to company goals. But most don't know how, and who can blame them? There's simply too much advice out there. Last year alone, more than 2,000 books on leadership were published, some of them even repackaging Moses and Shakespeare as leadership gurus. We've yet to hear advice that tells the whole truth about leadership. Yes, everyone agrees that leaders need vision, energy, authority, and strategic direction. That goes without saying. But we've discovered that inspirational leaders also share four unexpected qualities:

- **They selectively show their weaknesses.** By exposing some vulnerability, they reveal their approachability and humanity.

- **They rely heavily on intuition to gauge the appropriate timing and course of their actions.** Their ability to collect and interpret soft data helps them know just when and how to act.

- **They manage employees with something we call tough empathy.** Inspirational leaders empathize passionately—and realistically—with people, and they care intensely about the work employees do.

- **They reveal their differences.** They capitalize on what's unique about themselves.

You may find yourself in a top position without these qualities, but few people will want to be led by you.

Our theory about the four essential qualities of leadership, it should be noted, is not about results per se. While many of the leaders we have studied and use as examples do in fact post superior financial returns, the focus of our research has been on leaders who excel at inspiring people—in capturing hearts, minds, and souls. This ability is not everything in business, but any experienced leader will tell you it is worth quite a lot. Indeed, great results may be impossible without it.

Our research into leadership began some 25 years ago and has followed three streams since then. First, as academics, we ransacked the prominent leadership theories of the past century to develop our own working model of effective leadership. (For more on the history of leadership thinking, see "Leadership: A Small History of a Big Topic" at the end of this article.) Second, as consultants, we have tested our theory with thousands of executives in workshops worldwide and through observations with dozens of clients. And third, as executives ourselves, we have vetted our theories in our own organizations.

Some surprising results have emerged from our research. We learned that leaders need all four qualities to be truly inspirational; one or two qualities are rarely sufficient. Leaders who shamelessly promote their differences but who conceal their weaknesses, for instance, are usually ineffective—nobody wants a perfect leader. We also learned that the interplay between the four qualities is critical. Inspirational leaders tend to mix and match the qualities in order to find the right style for the right moment. Consider humor, which can be very effective as a difference. Used properly, humor can communicate a leader's charisma. But when a leader's sensing skills are not working, timing can be off and inappropriate humor can make someone seem like a joker or, worse, a fool. Clearly, in this case, being an effective leader means knowing what difference to use and when. And that's no mean feat, especially when the end result must be authenticity.

Reveal Your Weaknesses

When leaders reveal their weaknesses, they show us who they are—warts and all. This may mean admitting that they're irritable on Monday mornings, that they are somewhat disorganized, or even rather shy. Such admissions work because people need to see leaders own up to some flaw before they participate willingly in an endeavor. Exposing a weakness establishes trust and thus helps get folks on board. Indeed, if executives try to communicate that they're perfect at everything, there will be no need for anyone to help them with anything. They won't need followers. They'll signal that they can do it all themselves.

Beyond creating trust and a collaborative atmosphere, communicating a weakness also builds solidarity between followers and leaders. Consider a senior executive we know at a global management consultancy. He agreed to give a major presentation despite being badly afflicted by physical shaking caused by a medical condition. The otherwise highly critical audience greeted this courageous display of weakness with a standing ovation. By giving the talk, he had dared to say, "I am just like you—imperfect." Sharing an imperfection is so effective because it underscores a human being's authenticity. Richard Branson, the founder of Virgin, is a brilliant businessman and a hero in the United Kingdom. (Indeed, the Virgin brand is so linked to him personally that succession is a significant issue.) Branson is particularly effective at communicating his vulnerability. He is ill at ease and fumbles incessantly when interviewed in public. It's a weakness, but it's Richard Branson. That's what revealing a weakness is all about: showing your followers that you are genuine and approachable—human and humane.

Another advantage to exposing a weakness is that it offers a leader valuable protection. Human nature being what it is, if you don't show some weakness, then observers may invent one for you. Celebrities and politicians have always known this. Often, they deliberately give the public something to talk about, knowing full well that if they don't, the newspapers will invent something even worse. Princess Diana may have aired her eating disorder in public, but she died with her reputation intact, indeed even enhanced.

That said, the most effective leaders know that exposing a weakness must be done carefully. They own up to *selective* weaknesses. Knowing which weakness to disclose is a highly honed art. The golden rule is never to expose a weakness that will be seen as a fatal flaw—by which we mean a flaw that jeopardizes central aspects of your professional role. Consider the new finance director of a major corporation. He can't suddenly confess that he's never understood discounted cash flow. A leader should reveal only a tangential flaw—and perhaps even several of them. Paradoxically, this admission will help divert attention away from major weaknesses.

Another well-known strategy is to pick a weakness that can in some ways be considered a strength, such as being a workaholic. When leaders expose these limited flaws, people won't see much of anything and little harm will come to them. There is an important caveat, however: if the leader's vulnerability is not perceived to be genuine, he won't gain anyone's support. Instead he will open himself up to derision and scorn. One scenario we saw repeatedly in our research was one in which a CEO feigns absentmindedness to conceal his inconsistency or even dishonesty. This is a sure way to alienate followers who will remember accurately what happened or what was said.

Become a Sensor

Inspirational leaders rely heavily on their instincts to know when to reveal a weakness or a difference. We call them good situation sensors, and by that we mean that they can collect and interpret soft data. They can sniff out the signals in the environment and sense what's going on without having anything spelled out for them. Franz Humer, the CEO of Roche, is a classic sensor. He is highly accomplished in detecting shifts in climate and ambience; he can read subtle cues and sense underlying currents of opinion that elude less perceptive people. Humer says he developed this skill as a tour guide in his mid-twenties when he was responsible for groups of 100 or more. "There was no salary, only tips," he explains. "Pretty soon, I knew how to hone in on particular groups. Eventually, I could predict within 10% how much I could earn from any particular group." Indeed, great sensors can easily gauge unexpressed feelings; they can very accurately judge whether relationships are working or not. The process is complex, and as anyone who has ever encountered it knows, the results are impressive.

Consider a human resources executive we worked with in a multinational entertainment company. One day he got news of a distribution problem in Italy that had the potential to affect the company's worldwide operations. As he was thinking about how to hide the information temporarily from the Paris-based CEO while he worked on a solution, the phone rang. It was the CEO saying, "Tell me, Roberto, what the hell's going on in Milan?" The CEO was already aware that something was wrong. How? He had his networks, of course. But in large part, he was gifted at detecting information that wasn't aimed at him. He could read the silences and pick up on nonverbal cues in the organization.

Sensing can create problems. In making fine judgments about how far they can go, leaders risk losing their followers.

Not surprisingly, the most impressive business leaders we have worked with are all very refined sensors. Ray van Schaik, the chairman of Heineken in the early 1990s, is a good example. Conservative and urbane, van Schaik's genius lay in his ability to read signals he received from colleagues and from Freddie Heineken, the third-generation family member who was "always there without being there." While some senior managers spent a lot of time second-guessing the major shareholder, van Schaik developed an ability to "just know" what Heineken wanted. This ability was based on many years of working with him on the Heineken board, but it was more than that—van Schaik could read Heineken even though they had very different personalities and didn't work together directly.

Success stories like van Schaik's come with a word of warning. While leaders must be great sensors, sensing can create problems. That's because in making fine judgments about how far they can go, leaders risk losing their followers. The political situation in Northern Ireland is a powerful example. Over the past two years, several leaders—David Trimble, Gerry Adams, and Tony Blair, together with George Mitchell—have taken unprecedented initiatives toward peace. At every step of the way, these leaders had to sense how far they could go without losing their electorates. In business, think of mergers and acquisitions. Unless organizational leaders and negotiators can convince their followers in a timely way that the move is positive, value and goodwill quickly erode. This is the situation recently faced by Vodafone and France Telecom in the sale and purchase of Orange.

There is another danger associated with sensing skills. By definition, sensing a situation involves projection—that state of mind whereby you attribute your own ideas to other people and things. When a person "projects," his thoughts may interfere with the truth. Imagine a radio that picks up any number of signals, many of which are weak and distorted. Situation sensing is like that; you can't always be sure what you're hearing because of all the static. The employee who sees her boss distracted and leaps to the conclusion that she is going to be fired is a classic example. Most skills become heightened under threat, but particularly during situation sensing. Such oversensitivity in a leader can be a recipe for disaster. For this reason, sensing capability must always be framed by reality testing. Even the most gifted sensor may need to validate his perceptions with a trusted adviser or a member of his inner team.

Practice Tough Empathy

Unfortunately, there's altogether too much hype nowadays about the idea that leaders *must* show concern for their teams. There's nothing worse than seeing a manager return from the latest interpersonal-skills training program with "concern" for others. Real leaders don't need a training program to convince their employees that they care. Real leaders empathize fiercely with the people they lead. They also care intensely about the work their employees do.

Consider Alain Levy, the former CEO of PolyGram. Although he often comes across as a rather aloof intellectual, Levy is well able to close the distance between himself and his followers. On one occasion, he helped some junior record executives in Australia choose singles off albums. Picking singles is a critical task in the music business: the selection of a song can make or break the album. Levy sat down with the young people and took on the work with passion. "You bloody idiots," he added his voice to the melee, "you don't know what the hell you're talking about; we always have a dance track first!" Within 24 hours, the story spread throughout the company; it was the best PR Levy ever got. "Levy really knows how to pick singles," people said. In fact, he knew how to identify with the work, and he knew how to enter his followers' world—one where strong, colorful language is the norm—to show them that he cared.

Clearly, as the above example illustrates, we do not believe that the empathy of inspirational leaders is the soft kind described in so much of the management literature. On the contrary, we feel that real leaders manage through a unique approach we call tough empathy. Tough empathy means giving people what they need, not what they want. Organizations like the Marine Corps and consulting firms specialize in tough empathy. Recruits are pushed to be the best that they can be; "grow or go" is the motto. Chris Satterwaite, the CEO of Bell Pottinger Communications and a former chief executive of several ad agencies, understands what tough empathy is all about. He adeptly handles the challenges of managing creative people while making tough decisions. "If I have to, I can be ruthless," he says. "But while they're with me, I promise my people that they'll learn."

At its best, tough empathy balances respect for the individual and for the task at hand. Attending to both, however, isn't easy, especially when the business is in survival mode. At such times, caring leaders have to give selflessly to the people around them and know when to pull back. Consider a situation at Unilever at a time when it was developing Persil Power, a detergent that eventually had to be removed from the market because it destroyed clothes that were laundered in it. Even though the product was showing early signs of trouble, CEO Niall FitzGerald stood by his troops. "That was the popular place to be, but I should not have been there," he says now. "I should have stood back, cool and detached, looked at the whole field, watched out for the customer." But caring with detachment is not easy, especially since, when done right, tough empathy is harder on you than on your employees. "Some theories of leadership make caring look effortless. It isn't," says Paulanne Mancuso, president and CEO of Calvin Klein Cosmetics. "You have to do things you don't want to do, and that's hard." It's tough to be tough.

Tough empathy also has the benefit of impelling leaders to take risks. When Greg Dyke took over at the BBC, his commercial competitors were able to spend substantially more on programs than the BBC could. Dyke quickly realized that in order to thrive in a digital world, the BBC needed to increase its expenditures. He explained this openly and directly to the staff. Once he had secured their buy-in, he began thoroughly restructuring the organization. Although many employees were let go, he was able to maintain people's commitment. Dyke attributed his success to his tough empathy with employees: "Once you have the people with you, you can make the difficult decisions that need to be made."

One final point about tough empathy: those more apt to use it are people who really care about something. And when people care deeply about something—anything—they're more likely to show their true selves. They will not only communicate authenticity, which is the precondition for leadership, but they will show that they are doing more than just playing a role. People do not commit to executives who merely live up to the obligations of their jobs. They want more. They want someone who cares passionately about the people and the work— just as they do.

Dare to Be Different

Another quality of inspirational leaders is that they capitalize on what's unique about themselves. In fact, using these differences to great advantage is the most important quality of the four we've mentioned. The most effective leaders deliberately use differences to keep a social distance. Even as they are drawing their followers close to them, inspirational leaders signal their separateness.

Often, a leader will show his differences by having a distinctly different dress style or physical appearance, but typically he will move on to distinguish himself through qualities like imagination, loyalty, expertise, or even a handshake. Anything can be a difference, but it is important to communicate it. Most people, however, are hesitant to communicate what's unique about themselves, and it can take years for them to be fully aware of what sets them apart. This is a serious disadvantage in a world where networking is so critical and where teams need to be formed overnight.

Some leaders know exactly how to take advantage of their differences. Take Sir John Harvey-Jones, the former CEO of ICI—what was once the largest manufacturing company in the United Kingdom. When he wrote his autobiography a few years ago, a British newspaper advertised the book with a sketch of Harvey-Jones. The profile had a moustache, long hair, and a loud tie. The drawing was in black and white, but everyone knew who it was. Of course, John Harvey-Jones didn't get to the top of ICI because of eye-catching ties and long hair. But he was very clever in developing differences that he exploited to show that he was adventurous, entrepreneurial, and unique—he was John Harvey-Jones. There are other people who aren't as aware of their differences but still use them to great effect. For instance, Richard Surface, former managing director of the UK-based Pearl Insurance, always walked the floor and overtook people, using his own pace as a means of communicating urgency. Still other leaders are fortunate enough to have colleagues point out their differences for them. As the BBC's Greg Dyke puts it, "My partner tells me, 'You do things instinctively that you don't understand. What I worry about is that in the process of understanding them you could lose them!'" Indeed, what emerged in our interviews is that most leaders start off not knowing what their differences are but eventually come to know—and use—them more effectively over time. Franz Humer at Roche, for instance, now realizes that he uses his emotions to evoke reactions in others.

Most of the differences we've described are those that tend to be apparent, either to the leader himself or to the colleagues around him. But there are differences that are more subtle but still have very powerful effects. For instance, David Prosser, the CEO of Legal and General, one of Europe's largest and most successful insurance companies, is an outsider. He is not a smooth city type; in fact, he comes from industrial South Wales. And though generally approachable, Prosser has a hard edge, which he uses in an understated but highly effective way. At a recent cocktail party, a rather

Executives can over-differentiate themselves in their determination to express their separateness.

excitable sales manager had been claiming how good the company was at cross-selling products. In a low voice, Prosser intervened: "We may be good, but we're not good enough." A chill swept through the room. What was Prosser's point? Don't feel so close you can relax! I'm the leader, and I make that call. Don't you forget it. He even uses this edge to good effect with the top team—it keeps everyone on their toes.

Inspirational leaders use separateness to motivate others to perform better. It is not that they are being Machiavellian but that they recognize instinctively that followers will push themselves if their leader is just a little aloof. Leadership, after all, is not a popularity contest.

One danger, of course, is that executives can overdifferentiate themselves in their determination to express their separateness. Indeed, some leaders lose contact with their followers, and doing so is fatal. Once they create too much distance, they stop being good sensors, and they lose the ability to identify and care. That's what appeared to happen during Robert Horton's tenure as chairman and CEO of BP during the early 1990s. Horton's conspicuous display of his considerable—indeed, daunting—intelligence sometimes led others to see him as arrogant and self-aggrandizing. That resulted in overdifferentiation, and it eventually contributed to Horton's dismissal just three years after he was appointed to the position.

Leadership in Action

All four of the qualities described here are necessary for inspirational leadership, but they cannot be used mechanically. They must become or must already be part of an executive's personality. That's why the "recipe" business books—those that prescribe to the Lee Iaccoca or Bill Gates way—often fail. No one can just ape another leader. So the challenge facing prospective leaders is for them to be themselves, but with more skill. That can be done by making yourself increasingly aware of the four leadership qualities we describe and by manipulating these qualities to come up with a personal style that works for you. Remember, there is no universal formula, and what's needed will vary from context to context. What's more, the results are often subtle, as the following story about Sir Richard Sykes, the highly successful chairman and CEO of Glaxo Wellcome, one of the world's leading pharmaceutical companies, illustrates.

When he was running the R&D division at Glaxo, Sykes gave a year-end review to the company's top scientists. At the end of the presentation, a researcher asked him about one of the company's new compounds, and the two men engaged in a short heated debate. The question-answer session continued for another 20 minutes, at the end of which the researcher broached the subject again. "Dr. Sykes," he began in a loud voice, "you have still failed to understand the structure of the new compound." You could feel Sykes's temper rise through the soles of his feet. He marched to the back of the room and displayed his anger before the intellectual brainpower of the entire company. "All right, lad," he yelled, "let us have a look at your notes!"

The Sykes story provides the ideal framework for discussing the four leadership qualities. To some people, Sykes's irritability could have seemed like inappropriate weakness. But in this context, his show of temper demonstrated Sykes's deep belief in the discussion about basic science—a company value. Therefore, his willingness to get angry actually cemented his credibility as a leader. He also showed that he was a very good sensor. If Sykes had exploded earlier in the meeting, he would have quashed the debate. Instead, his anger was perceived as defending the faith. The story also reveals Sykes's ability to identify with his colleagues and their work. By talking to the researcher as a fellow scientist, he was able to create an empathic bond with his audience. He really cared, though his caring was clearly tough empathy. Finally, the story indicates Sykes's own willingness to show his differences. Despite being one of the United Kingdom's most successful businessmen, he has not conformed to "standard" English. On the contrary, Sykes proudly retains his distinctive northern accent. He also doesn't show the typical British reserve and decorum; he radiates passion. Like other real leaders, he acts and communicates naturally. Indeed, if we were to sum up the entire year-end review at Glaxo Wellcome, we'd say that Sykes was being himself—with great skill.

Unraveling the Mystery

As long as business is around, we will continue to pick apart the underlying ingredients of true leadership. And there will always be as many theories as there are questions. But of all the facets of leadership that one might investigate, there are few so difficult as understanding what it takes to develop leaders. The four leadership qualities are a necessary first step. Taken together, they tell executives to be authentic. As we counsel the executives we coach: "Be yourselves—more—with skill." There can be no advice more difficult to follow than that.

Leadership: A Small History of a Big Topic

PEOPLE HAVE BEEN TALKING about leadership since the time of Plato. But in organizations all over the world— in dinosaur conglomerates and new-economy start-ups alike—the same complaint emerges: we don't have enough leadership. We have to ask ourselves, Why are we so obsessed with leadership?

One answer is that there is a crisis of belief in the modern world that has its roots in the rationalist revolution of the eighteenth century. During the Enlightenment, philosophers such as Voltaire claimed that through the application of reason alone, people could control their destiny. This marked an incredibly optimistic turn in world history. In the nineteenth century, two beliefs stemmed from this rationalist notion: a belief in progress and a belief in the perfectibility of man. This produced an even rosier world view than before. It wasn't until the end of the nineteenth century, with the writings first of Sigmund Freud and later of Max Weber, that the chinks in the armor appeared. These two thinkers destroyed Western man's belief in rationality and progress. The current quest for leadership is a direct consequence of their work.

The founder of psychoanalysis, Freud theorized that beneath the surface of the rational mind was the unconscious. He supposed that the unconscious was responsible for a fair proportion of human behavior. Weber, the leading critic of Marx and a brilliant sociologist, also explored the limits of reason. Indeed, for him, the most destructive force operating in institutions was something he called technical rationality—that is, rationality without morality.

For Weber, technical rationality was embodied in one particular organizational form—the bureaucracy. Bureaucracies, he said, were frightening not for their inefficiencies but for their efficiencies and their capacity to dehumanize people. The tragic novels of Franz Kafka bear stark testimony to the debilitating effects of bureaucracy. Even more chilling was the testimony of Hitler's lieutenant Adolf Eichmann that "I was just a good bureaucrat." Weber believed that the only power that could resist bureaucratization was charismatic leadership. But even this has a very mixed record in the twentieth century. Although there have been inspirational and transformational wartime leaders, there have also been charismatic leaders like Hitler, Stalin, and Mao Tse-tung who committed horrendous atrocities.

By the twentieth century, there was much skepticism about the power of reason and man's ability to progress continuously. Thus, for both pragmatic and philosophic reasons, an intense interest in the concept of leadership began to develop. And indeed, in the 1920s, the first serious research started. The first leadership theory—trait theory—attempted to identify the common characteristics of effective leaders. To that end, leaders were weighed and measured and subjected to a battery of psychological tests. But no one could identify what effective leaders had in common. Trait theory fell into disfavor soon after expensive studies concluded that effective leaders were either above-average height or below.

Trait theory was replaced by style theory in the 1940s, primarily in the United States. One particular style of leadership was singled out as having the most potential. It was a hail-fellow-well-met democratic style of leadership, and thousands of American executives were sent to training courses to learn how to behave this way.

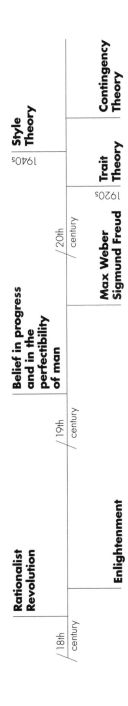

There was only one drawback. The theory was essentially capturing the spirit of FDR's America—open, democratic, and meritocratic. And so when McCarthyism and the Cold War surpassed the New Deal, a completely new style was required. Suddenly, everyone was encouraged to behave like a Cold War warrior! The poor executive was completely confused.

Recent leadership thinking is dominated by contingency theory, which says that leadership is dependent on a particular situation. That's fundamentally true, but given that there are endless contingencies in life, there are endless varieties of leadership. Once again, the beleaguered executive looking for a model to help him is hopelessly lost.

For this article, we ransacked all the leadership theories to come up with the four essential leadership qualities. Like Weber, we look at leadership that is primarily antibureaucratic and charismatic. From trait theory, we derived the qualities of weaknesses and differences. Unlike the original trait theorists, however, we do not believe that all leaders have the same weaknesses; our research only showed that all leaders expose some flaws. Tough empathy grew out of style theory, which looked at different kinds of relationships between leaders and their followers. Finally, context theory set the stage for needing to know what skills to use in various circumstances.

Four Popular Myths About Leadership

In both our research and consulting work, we have seen executives who profoundly misunderstand what makes an inspirational leader. Here are four of the most common myths:

Everyone can be a leader.

Not true. Many executives don't have the self-knowledge or the authenticity necessary for leadership. And self-knowledge and authenticity are only part of the equation. Individuals must also want to be leaders, and many talented employees are not interested in shouldering that responsibility. Others prefer to devote more time to their private lives than to their work. After all, there is more to life than work, and more to work than being the boss.

Leaders deliver business results.

Not always. If results were always a matter of good leadership, picking leaders would be easy. In every case, the best strategy would be to go after people in companies with the best results. But clearly, things are not that simple. Businesses in quasi-monopolistic industries can often do very well with competent management rather than great leadership. Equally, some well-led businesses do not necessarily produce results, particularly in the short term.

People who get to the top are leaders.

Not necessarily. One of the most persistent misperceptions is that people in leadership positions are leaders. But people who make it to the top may have done so because of political acumen, not necessarily because of true leadership quality. What's more, real leaders are found all over the organization, from the executive suite to the shop floor. By definition, leaders are simply people who have followers, and rank doesn't have much to do with that. Effective military organizations like the U.S. Navy have long realized the importance of developing leaders throughout the organization.

Leaders are great coaches.

Rarely. A whole cottage industry has grown up around the teaching that good leaders ought to be good coaches. But that thinking assumes that a single person can both inspire the troops and impart technical skills. Of course, it's possible that great leaders may also be great coaches, but we see that only occasionally. More typical are leaders like Steve Jobs whose distinctive strengths lie in their ability to excite others through their vision rather than through their coaching talents.

Can Female Leaders Be True to Themselves?

GENDER DIFFERENCES CAN be used to either positive or negative effect. Women, in particular, are prone to being stereotyped according to differences—albeit usually not the ones that they would choose. Partly this is because there are fewer women than men in management positions. According to research in social psychology, if a group's representation falls below 20% in a given society, then it's going to be subjected to stereotyping whether it likes it or not. For women, this may mean being typecast as a "helper," "nurturer," or "seductress"—labels that may prevent them from defining their own differences.

In earlier research, we discovered that many women—particularly women in their fifties—try to avoid this dynamic by disappearing. They try to make themselves invisible. They wear clothes that disguise their bodies; they try to blend in with men by talking tough. That's certainly one way to avoid negative stereotyping, but the problem is that it reduces a woman's chances of being seen as a potential leader. She's not promoting her real self and differences.

Another response to negative stereotyping is to collectively resist it—for example, by mounting a campaign that promotes the rights, opportunities, and even the number of women in the workplace. But on a day-to-day basis, survival is often all women have time for, therefore making it impossible for them to organize themselves formally.

A third response that emerged in our research was that women play into stereotyping to personal advantage. Some women, for example, knowingly play the role of "nurturer" at work, but they do it with such wit and skill that they are able to benefit from it. The cost of such a strategy? It furthers harmful stereotypes and continues to limit opportunities for other women to communicate their genuine personal differences.

Originally published in September–October 2000
Reprint R00506

Leading Through Rough Times

An Interview with Novell's Eric Schmidt

BRONWYN FRYER

Executive Summary

FEW LARGE COMPANIES HAVE soared as high, sunk as low, and struggled as long as the 18-year-old networking software maker Novell. For years, the company dominated the market for local area networks, but by 1997, it had faltered due to misguided acquisitions, product missteps, and large unsold inventories. That's when Eric Schmidt arrived from Sun Microsystems to take over as Novell's third CEO.

He turned the company around with a deft combination of cost reductions, divestitures, and new product rollouts, and by 1998, it was back in the black. Unfortunately, the good times didn't last, and like most technology companies, Novell is once again struggling with a slowdown in demand.

But Schmidt is optimistic about returning Novell to good health, and his strategies suggest ways for other organizations to handle themselves during downturns. He counsels against being overly cautious during such times. It may be necessary to eliminate excess inventory, cut costs, and reduce the size of the staff and the management team in order to stabilize a company. Working to retain those employees whom he calls the "smart people" and keeping them motivated will have long-term payoffs.

Further, Schmidt says it is necessary to acknowledge and overcome a "culture of fear," the deadening environment of cynicism in which employees suppress thoughts and feelings because they're worried about layoffs. His additional advice: keep new products coming out to sustain the interest of customers and the press, pay attention to your cash position, stay focused on your desired outcomes, and take heart from other industry leaders.

Few large companies have soared as high, sunk as low, and struggled as long as the 18-year-old networking software maker Novell. Not long after it was founded in Provo, Utah, in 1983, the company came to dominate the market for local area networks. But after several misguided acquisitions and product missteps in the mid-1990s, Novell seemed to be down for the count in April 1997. That's when Eric Schmidt, the highly respected CTO at Sun Microsystems, surprised the business world by accepting an offer to become the beleaguered company's third CEO as well as its chairman. His mandate: put Novell back onto a sound financial footing, refocus it on its core engineering strengths, and turn it into a leading player in Internet software and network services.

The situation Schmidt faced was daunting, to say the least. Microsoft, with its Windows NT operating system, was competing aggressively for the networking market. Novell was saddled with an outdated product line and large unsold inventories. Customers were getting nervous, and reporters were beginning to write the company's obituary. With a deft combination of cost reductions, divestitures, and new product rollouts, Schmidt turned the company around. By 1998, it was back in the black. But the good times didn't last long. Like most technology companies, Novell is now struggling with a slowdown in demand. And in March, the company announced its intentions to acquire Cambridge Technology Partners and to appoint Jack Messman, current CEO of CTP, as CEO of Novell. Now acting as Novell's chief strategist, Schmidt is back in turnaround mode.

It's a mode that seems to suit him. In February, when he sat down in Novell's executive offices in San Jose, California, for this interview, he talked expansively about the challenges involved in bringing a once proud company back to life and then leading it through yet another tough stretch. When you enter a downturn, he said, you have to fight the instinct to be overly cautious. Rather, you have to encourage your most creative people to take chances, to follow their hunches. The alternative is to succumb to a "culture of fear," in which a bleak vision of the future becomes a self-fulfilling prophecy.

In today's unpredictable business world, with its ever shifting markets and competitors, the prospect of a sudden downturn haunts every executive. Eric Schmidt's experience provides more than a cautionary tale; it suggests a path through the wilderness.

*A lot of people were stunned when you left Sun for
Novell in 1997. Why did you make the move? And what
did you find when you arrived?*

I had spent a long time—14 years—in a variety of executive positions at Sun, and I'd hit the top of my game as CTO. I was ready to try something new. Over time, I'd become fascinated by network technology, and Novell looked like a good fit with my interests. When I agreed to take the job, I'd done my homework. McKinsey had performed an audit and reported that the company had lots of cash. Novell's main product, NetWare, was a solid brand. I knew that I was coming to an organization that needed help, but I certainly didn't think it was hopeless.

Things were considerably worse than I expected. On my first day on the job, the president told me that it looked like our revenues would be up $20 million for the quarter. That was terrific news. But on day three, he caught me in the hallway. He was ashen. "We have a problem," he said. "Remember what I told you about being up $20 million? Well, it turns out we're actually down $20 million." Our sales were tanking, and we had a lot of inventory backed up in the channel. It was a shock, to say the least.

A few days later, I found myself on a plane sitting next to Roel Pieper, the former CEO of Tandem Computers, which had recently been acquired by Compaq. I told Roel about my problem. He smiled at me and said, "Congratulations. You're about to do a turnaround."

"Are you kidding?" I said. "That's not at all what I signed up for."

"Nonetheless, that's what you're going to do," Roel informed me. "And I can help you. First, you do a big layoff."

"But I didn't come here to fire people."

"Second, you get rid of 80% of your executives."

"You've got to be kidding."

"And," he said, "you do all this in the next three weeks."

"I can't possibly terminate people I haven't met yet," I said. And then I asked myself, "What on earth have I gotten into?"

In my third week on the job, we had to decide what to tell Wall Street regarding our revenue loss. The CFO told me that we had enough revenue reserves, despite high inventory in the distribution channel, to avoid preannouncing the shortfall. But that strategy made me nervous. I knew that a lot of software companies had run into trouble with the SEC for questionable accounting tricks. I called the cochairman, John Young (the former CEO of Hewlett-Packard), to seek his advice, and he asked me, "What does your gut say?" I said that I felt we should be honest and announce the shortfall. And John said, "I approve." Later, he told me that he knew then that he'd made the right decision in hiring me. But after that announcement, everyone really thought the company was dead as a doornail.

After you got over the shock, how did you go about bringing Novell back to life?

First, of course, you have to stop the bleeding and stabilize the patient. And that requires exactly the kind of tough, fast action Roel Pieper had described. We had what I call a "kitchen sink" quarter, when you clean up the mess. We drained the excess inventory from the channel and cut costs drastically. We laid off more than 1,000 employees and replaced most of the executive management team, reducing seven layers of management to four. Those were painful steps, but they were necessary to save the company. At the same time, I met personally with our major customers to show them what we were doing and to convince them that we were still alive. And we launched an aggressive PR campaign, announcing new products or product upgrades every month. The trade press is crucial in our business, and we had to get the word out that we were moving forward.

While we were making these kinds of tactical moves, we were also repositioning the company strategically and refocusing on our core networking strengths. But neither the cost cutting nor the repositioning represented the biggest challenge we faced when I joined Novell. The biggest challenge was retaining our key talent—the ones I call the "smart people"—and keeping them motivated. A company can survive losing a lot of people, but if it loses its smart people, it's done for.

Keeping your most talented employees must have been particularly difficult given the company's precarious condition. What did you do?

The first thing I had to do was identify them. In a company like ours that is driven by innovation, you can't just look at an org chart to find your most important employees. The key people here are our most creative engineers—they're the smart people, the ones who control our future—and they can be very well hidden in the organization. They're not necessarily at the top of any hierarchy.

I used a kind of algorithm to locate these people. A few days after I started, I was on the company shuttle from San Jose to Provo, where our engineering staff is centered, and I was sitting knee-to-knee with two engineers embroiled in a fascinating, heated argument. They were obviously two extremely bright people. I asked them to give me the names of the smartest people they knew in the company. They gave me a list, and over the next week I set up half-hour meetings with all of those other smart people, and I asked each of them to give me the names of the ten smartest people they knew. Because the smart people in an organization tend to know one another, I eventually found out who they were—about 100 in all.

I met and talked with each of them. It helped that, as an engineer myself, I understood their intellectual and technological needs and what their concerns were. I listened intently while they told me about their experiences and their frustrations. They were very demoralized; no one had listened to them for a long time, and they had basically decided to lie low and keep their mouths shut. As a result, lots of great ideas were being lost.

The more conversations I had, the more clear it became that Novell had a dysfunctional culture, a sick culture. Doctors will tell you that when you're sick, having a diagnosis allows you to focus your energy on overcoming your disease. So my management team worked together to name Novell's condition, and we ended up calling it the "culture of fear." In a culture of fear, which I think is a common condition in companies going through rough times, people are always worried about getting laid off, and so they suppress their feelings. Instead of complaining to their bosses, whom they fear might fire them, they

It's a natural reaction to turn cautious when your company's in trouble, but that's precisely the wrong tack to take.

complain vociferously to their peers. That's what was going on here. This situation created a kind of pervasive bellyaching, a corporate cynicism. A related condition, which we came to call the "Novell nod," was ubiquitous. People would sit in a room, listening to someone talk and nodding in agreement. Then, as they left the room, they'd all say to one another, "That was the stupidest thing I've ever heard." I'd see that kind of behavior constantly.

So exactly how do you overcome a culture of fear?

You begin by recognizing that you can't change a culture by fiat. The problem lies deep within the organization, and you have to give everyone—not just the smart people—permission to correct it. In our case, that meant encouraging people to say what was really on their minds. I remember one instance of this, in a meeting with a group of engineers. There was something wrong with the meeting's atmosphere: it was a little too controlled, a little too formal. I kept asking questions, pushing for an answer. And finally, one of the engineers exploded, saying, "I can't take this!" We were all a little shocked. Then he looked at me and said, "Do I have permission to be passionate?" I said, "Yes, of course!" Then he stood up and gave this incredibly lucid proposal for a new product. He'd been so constrained by the culture that he'd been afraid to promote his idea for fear of being shot down by his boss.

I spent a lot of time trying to get people to open up in this way, to give voice to the ideas they'd buried inside themselves. Some of these ideas were brilliant, and I encouraged people to work on them. You know, it's a natural reaction to turn cautious when your company's in trouble, but that's precisely the wrong tack to take. You have to give people freedom to pursue their passions. That's the only way to keep them focused and inspired and to ensure you'll have a flow of new products to regain, retain, or grow ground in the market. The new version of our flagship product, NetWare 5.0, emerged in this way. After we released it in September 1998, our revenues improved nicely, leading to after-tax profits of $192 million on revenues of $1.3 billion in 1999. This built on improvement from the preceding fiscal year when our after-tax profits were $102 million on revenues of $1.1 billion, compared with a loss of $78 million on $1 billion of revenue in 1997. The turnaround wouldn't have been so dramatic if we'd told people to be careful.

Another way to overcome a culture of fear is to show employees that you understand what the cultural problems are and that you are committed to fixing them. Sales meetings, for example, offer opportunities not only to motivate people and get them excited about new products or directions but also to address cultural issues on a broad scale. At one meeting, I told the audience that we had discovered a secret weapon deep in the bowels of Provo. And I introduced this engineer in a Hawaiian shirt named Ron Tanner. Ron launched into a very funny story about how the management in California has never understood anything and how a few engineers in Utah pulled together as a team and developed this brilliant product for customers. Everything he said resonated with the audience, who were laughing and shouting, "Yeah!" Then he unveiled the product, ZENworks, the first new product developed under my leadership. This product had long been suppressed within the culture of fear, but Ron and his team succeeded in bringing it out. ZENworks now produces more than $100 million in revenues for us. That sales meeting was a wonderful public acknowledgment that there had been suppression—a kind of denial about things like the friction between the Utah people and the California people—but that now the era of suppression was over.

I'm not saying we're completely cured, by the way. The cultural issues have been extremely difficult to eradicate. In fact, I'm less satisfied about this today than I was two years ago. When I first arrived here, I experienced an incredible outpouring of goodwill, as if I'd ridden in on a white horse. But cultural problems are like cancer. They keep coming back. So I still feel the remnants of the culture of fear, and I still sometimes see the Novell nod. The good news is that these problems don't appear in gross forms the way they used to, and, when they do appear, we know how to address them.

Despite the cultural problems, you've had good luck in keeping employees from jumping ship. Novell's turnover rate in 1998–99 hovered around 15%, which was significantly lower than the industry average of 22%. How have you kept people, particularly the smart people, from leaving?

A lot of it is Management 101: repeating the same message 20 times, training the trainers, getting in front of people, cheering them on. We're also fortunate to have our engineering headquarters in Utah, where the competition for talent is much less fierce than in Silicon Valley. We do whatever it takes to hang on to our top talent. Sometimes that includes counteroffers. Most people will tell you that's a bad idea, because extending a counteroffer leads to bidding wars. But when you lose a talented marketing person to the competition, it's a huge cost to your business because great knowledge and skills go to a competitor. Usually, when we ask people why they're leaving, they talk about money. But most of the time, it's something else, like a project or a manager or their confidence in the company. We pay attention to compensation issues but then also work on the real issues of management and leadership.

In addition, you need some kind of early warning system so that you always have a chance to get to people before they're out the door. In a company in difficulty, you can't presume that people are happy. So I've told my staff to sit down every day with everyone who reports to them and ask overtly how they're doing and if they're happy. That forces people to discuss their concerns. Most of them will be honest if you give them the opportunity, I've found.

I've found that the best way to manage smart people is to let them self-organize so they can operate both inside and outside the management hierarchy.

Retaining people is only one facet of the challenge, though. You also have to keep them motivated, and smart people are not as motivated by money as they are by recognition. At Novell, we have something called the President's Award Program, an annual dinner at which we recognize individual accomplishments. We choose 20 of our top employees each year, and we invite them and their spouses to the dinner and give them plaques and stock option grants to recognize their accomplishments. These are simple gestures, but it's amazing what they do for people. Recognition like this makes it much harder for them to leave the company, and it keeps them much more engaged in their work.

Smart people also need to feel that they are part of the solution. Most companies make the mistake of putting their most creative people in places where their contributions are limited or where they're resented by others. If you put them in research, they're ghettoized. If you put them in product groups, no one likes them because they work differently than everyone else. If you put them in strategy jobs, they write wonderful documents that no one uses. And in a hierarchical company, you have some managers who are not as smart as the people who work for them. These managers act like colonels. They tell the smart person, "Take the hill!," and the smart person says, "But I've been thinking about this and—" And the colonel says, "No. Take the hill!" That kind of command and control does not work.

I've found that the best way to manage smart people is to let them self-organize so they can operate both inside and outside the management hierarchy. They report to a manager, but they also have the latitude to work on projects that interest them, regardless of whether they originate with their own manager. You tell them, "Look, I don't know how to solve this problem, so why don't you throw yourself at it and figure it out? Take the time and resources you need, and get it right." If they get frustrated and need to blow off steam, you invite them to talk to you directly—no go-betweens. At the same time, you discuss this new component of the person's work directly with his or her manager, and there are no reprisals when a smart person works outside a manager's jurisdiction. It's the complete opposite of the culture of fear.

To win the hearts and minds of your key employees, you have to communicate directly and physically with them. Videoconferencing, telephone, e-mail, and other tools don't cut it. Politicians use the handclasp, and so do the best industry leaders. Since I've been here, I've spent way too much time on our corporate jet. In the beginning, I routinely hit five cities a day. That lifestyle is grueling but utterly necessary. Eighty percent of winning is just showing up.

Rarely is a corporate culture embedded only in a company's people; it also tends to be embedded in the processes and systems of the company. Was that the case at Novell?

Yes, and it was a big problem. For example, we had to change our reward systems to make sure people stayed focused on our key objectives, and we had to do it in a very short time frame. When I first came to Novell, our salespeople knew that they were spending too much time selling through the channel and not enough selling directly to corporate customers. This practice led to huge inventory problems, which were very costly to us. So we set up quarterly objectives for direct selling, and we also introduced a new incentive program based on 25 points: if you earned at least 20 points, based on the fulfillment of your objectives, you got a 100% bonus at the end of the quarter. When people would come to me and complain—which they always did—I would ask, "What are your objectives for this quarter?" If they didn't know them, I'd call their bosses and make sure they knew that the objectives had to be clearly communicated down the line. Business as usual wasn't going to cut it.

Incidentally, not all systemic changes work. I've also learned that certain management techniques can actually make things worse when applied to a distressed culture. For example, I had always worked in companies with yearly and quarterly employee ranking systems, in which people were divided into three groups: overperforming, performing, and underperforming. So not long after I came here, we started a ranking program that graded on a curve: 45% into the overperforming group, 50% into the performing group, and 5% into the underperforming group. I didn't know—and certainly didn't intend it this way—that if you got the lowest grade, it was presumed that you were about to be fired. We started getting hate mail from people who argued that there was no way to rank people who worked as a team. The ranking system exacerbated the culture of fear and proved to be such a huge retention and motivation issue that we were forced to stop it after a year. In its place, we introduced a modified ranking program that better reflected overall employee performance.

Novell had a resurgence through 1999, so your efforts obviously paid off. But like many companies, particularly in the tech sector, it's now facing slackening demand, rapid technological change, and relentless competition. How do you keep the company buoyant through the ups and downs?

First of all, we take our cash position very, very seriously. I balance my personal checkbook to the penny every month, and we run the company in the same way—as if the cash were our personal money. My first rule of business is that when you run out of cash, you close the doors. Cash is the last bulwark. That's a simple rule, but it's one that executives too often forget. I was fortunate to learn it when Sun nearly ran out of cash in 1989. The

CFO had to get a bank loan to keep the company afloat. So after we turned around Novell, I was careful to harvest assets. The goal was to collect cash, hoard it, manage it, and talk about it a lot.

Harvesting cash is particularly tricky for companies in distress, because that's when customers don't pay. We put in a set of objectives for the sales force based on cash collection, and we made it a point to get everybody thinking about saving money. That discipline is helping us in our current transition away from our packaged software and toward our new technology platform. Our sales are under pressure at the moment, but our balance sheet is in incredibly good shape. We have almost no inventory in the channel, more than $700 million in cash, strong positive cash flow from operations, and hundreds of millions in investments that, we hope, will generate more cash down the road. Our cash position allows us to go on as we are for a long, long time, but we expect revenues to grow again in 2002.

Reporters and stock analysts can be brutal on a CEO when a company goes through a downturn. What keeps you from getting discouraged? What gives you the perspective to keep leading Novell through difficult times?

Obviously, I have very good reasons for putting up with four years of turning around a business and struggling to make it successful in new markets. First, I actually like the network services space that Novell is in. We have an immense market opportunity in this area. As for those greatly exaggerated rumors of Novell's death, I try to take them in stride while working hard to educate the market about our real situation. You know, it's easy to sit on the outside and criticize the one who's making the decisions. Taking harsh criticism is part of any top executive's job. Real leadership involves taking the heat and staying focused on the way to achieve the desired outcome. Look at Steve Case. In 1997, he decided to change AOL's pricing to a flat $21 per month. He shouldered unbelievable criticism for that. I remember being on a panel with him at the time, and he was introduced as the "most hated CEO in America." They played a busy signal as he walked onstage. And he came out and said to the audience, "I'm sorry, I'm sorry. We're doing everything we can to get this right. But this is the decision we've made, and this strategy is the right one." Today, AOL is incredibly successful. No one doubts now that Steve was right, but everybody doubted him back then.

When you fly a plane, as complicated as it is, there are only a few things that will kill you. You can run out of gas, fly too low, or go off course. In my world, it's a good metaphor.

It helps that business leaders understand what their colleagues are experiencing and go out of their way to support one another. I'm fortunate to have lots of good relationships with the tech industry's leaders, many of whom I met when I was Sun's CTO. I recall a moment in May 2000 when Novell was forced to preannounce a bad quarter. That very afternoon, Steve Jobs called me and said, "I wanted you to know that I know what you're going through, but I respect what you're doing and I wish you the best of luck." The next call was from Dave Wetherell of CMGI, which has had ups and downs, too. He told me, "These things are hard, but you have to stick with your principles, stay with your focus, and you will win." I believe these people. In fact, I think people trust leaders who have toughed it out through crises more than those who've had easy sailing. In a way, the fact that Novell has gone through crises has made me a more credible leader. I'm still here, and I'm still fighting for the company.

One thing that helps me a lot—that keeps things in perspective—is flying. I'm a commercial pilot, and during my most recent training, I was doing a difficult maneuver called "circle to land." I was in a twin-engine plane, and I was wearing a kind of hood so that I couldn't see out the windows. The instructor had shut down half the instruments and one engine, and I had to fly by the few remaining indicators. Then, at 900 feet, the control tower switched the runway on me. I had to turn around within a mile and come in on the other runway. I did the maneuver successfully. When you fly a plane, as complicated as it is, there are only a few things that will kill you. You can run out of gas, fly too low, or go off course. In my world, it's a good metaphor. As long as we pay attention to the important things, we'll survive.

Back to the Network

AFTER NOVELL WAS FOUNDED in 1983, its flagship product, NetWare, quickly became the de facto standard in operating system software for local area networks (LANs). But in the 1990s, two epochal events combined to undermine the company's leadership position. First, in late 1993, Microsoft entered the networking market with its Windows NT operating system. Second, the rise of the Internet created a powerful new standard for networking, rendering the old LAN architecture obsolete. Faced with an erosion of its core market, Novell launched an ill-fated diversification initiative, spending $1.5 billion to acquire packaged-software businesses such as WordPerfect Corporation to compete with Microsoft on the desktop. Thus distracted, Novell saw its grip on the networking market slip further, even as its new products failed to live up to the company's overly optimistic expectations.

Since taking over as chairman and CEO in 1997, Eric Schmidt has pulled Novell back to its networking roots while also guiding the company into the booming market for Internet-based products and services. At the core of Schmidt's strategy is a new product called eDirectory (founded on the Novell Directory Services platform). This software allows corporate IT departments to hold down the operational costs associated with locating and managing millions of "objects"—servers, PCs, notebooks, wireless devices, routers, application programs, files, and users—on ever expanding networks composed of complicated and diverse mini-networks. By developing and selling applications and services that take advantage of the eDirectory system and that operate across all computing platforms, Schmidt believes Novell can become a leader in the rapidly growing directory-services market.

The company's fortunes initially rebounded in 1999 with the successful launch of NetWare 5.0, its new, industrial-strength network operating system. And customers appear to be embracing the eDirectory system, opening up many new opportunities for the company. Indeed, the fastest growing segment of its business is applications such as ZENworks and GroupWise, built to run on eDirectory.

But Novell is not out of the woods yet. In 2000, corporate technology spending began to slow, and Novell's revenues, like those of many high-tech companies, flattened. In March 2001, the company announced plans to acquire Cambridge Technology Partners, a global IT service provider, accelerating Novell's shift into services. As part of the acquisition, CTP CEO Jack Messman will succeed Schmidt as CEO of Novell. Schmidt will continue as the company's chairman and will also become its chief strategist.

Originally published in May 2001
Reprint R0105H

About the Contributors

JOHN C. BECK is Associate Partner and Director of Research at Accenture's Institute for Strategic Change, Palo Alto. He is also a visiting professor at the Anderson School of Management at the University of California at Los Angeles and an adjunct professor at the Ivey School at the University of Western Ontario. Beck has served as Publisher of *The Asian Century* newsletter and has published more than one hundred books, articles, and business reports on topics of e-commerce, business in Asia, strategic management, globalization, leadership, and organizational behavior.

DAN CIAMPA is an advisor to CEOs and other senior leaders who must improve overall organizational performance and change corporate culture for sustainability. He was Chairman and CEO of Rath & Strong, Inc., from 1984 to 1996. In twenty-five years there, he consulted on leadership challenges and operations improvement with leading manufacturing, consumer packaged goods, financial services, and pharmaceutical companies. He led the first successful integration of organization development and technical problem solving, participated in the introduction of total quality management and lean manufacturing to the United States, and chaired cross-industry collaboration groups such as the Automation Forum. He serves on the boards of seven organizations including Delta Rubber Company, Union College, National Public Radio

Foundation, and the American Health Foundation. He is the author of three books and numerous articles. His most recent book is *Right from the Start*, published in 1999.

THOMAS H. DAVENPORT is Director of Accenture Institute for Strategic Change, a research center in Cambridge, Massachusetts. He is also Distinguished Scholar in Residence at Babson College. He is the author of nine books including *The Attention Economy*, coauthored with John Beck; *Mission Critical*, *Working Knowledge*, coauthored with Laurence Prusak; and *Process Innovation*. He has written over a hundred articles on the roles of information, knowledge, and technology in contemporary business.

BRONWYN FRYER is a senior editor at *Harvard Business Review*.

ROBERT GOFFEE is Professor of Organisational Behaviour at London Business School. He also serves as Deputy Dean for Executive Education, Director of the Innovation Exchange, and a member of the Governing Body. Previously, he was Director of the Accelerated Development Programme and Chair of the Organisational Behaviour Group. Professor Goffee has led significant executive development initiatives in Europe, North America, and Asia. His work has covered a range of industries with a focus on leadership, change, and corporate performance. His clients have included Heineken, Roche, Sonae, KPMG, Unilever, and MLIM. He has published nine books and over fifty articles in the areas of entrepreneurship, managerial careers, organization design, and corporate culture. These include *Entrepreneurship in Europe*, *Reluctant Managers*, *Corporate Realities*, and *The Character of a Corporation*. "Why Should Anyone Be Led by You?" won the McKinsey Award for best article published in 2000. He is Founding Partner of Creative Management Associates, which consults to major international companies around the world in the areas of change management, top teams, and organizational development.

DANIEL GOLEMAN is the author of the best-selling books *Emotional Intelligence* and *Working with Emotional Intelligence*, and coauthor of the forthcoming *Leading with Emotional Intelligence*. A trained psychologist, he worked for many years for the *New York Times* covering the brain and behavioral sciences. He has also been a visiting faculty member at Harvard University. Dr. Goleman is co-chair of the Consortium for Research on Emotional Intelligence in Organizations at Rutgers University, and a founder of the Collaborative for Social and Emotional Learning at the University of Illinois at Chicago. Through an affiliation with the HayGroup he consults on leadership and organizational development worldwide.

At the time this article was originally published, **GARETH JONES** was the director of human resources and international communications at the British Broadcasting Corporation and a former professor of organizational development at Henley Management College in Oxfordshire, England.

MICHAEL MACCOBY is an anthropologist and a psychoanalyst. He is also Founder and President of the Maccoby Group, a management consultancy in Washington, DC. The former director of the Program on Technology, Public Policy, and Human Development at Harvard University's Kennedy School of Government in Cambridge, Massachusetts, Maccoby is the author of *The Leader: A New Face for American Management*, *The Gamesman: The New Corporate Leaders*, and *Why Work? Motivating the New Workforce*.

JOHN PETERMAN was the chairman and CEO of the J. Peterman Company from 1987 to 1999.

MICHAEL WATKINS is Associate Professor of Business Administration at Harvard Business School. Prior to joining Harvard Business School, Professor Watkins was an associate professor of public policy at Harvard University's Kennedy School of Government, where he taught negotiation and persuasion and did research on international diplomacy and the management of organizational transformation. His current research focuses on corporate diplomacy, exploring how senior executives manage external relations with other business leaders, government officials, boards of directors, shareholders, analysts, and the media. He is the coauthor of *Right from the Start* and *Winning the Influence Game* and author of *Taking Charge in Your New Leadership Role*.

Index